WHATEVER IS, IS RIGHT.

BY

A. B. CHILD, M.D.

" All things work round like worlds. The orb of hell
Hath yet its place in heaven, as thine and all.
* * * spirit is the substance of all matter,
* * * * * in all existence.
Look at your spirit."

BOSTON:
BERRY, COLBY, & COMPANY.
3½ BRATTLE STREET.
1860.

STEREOTYPED BY COWLES AND COMPANY,
17 WASHINGTON ST., BOSTON.

Rand & Avery, Printers, 3 Cornhill, Boston.

PREFACE.

THIS book aims to speak of life as it is. It has approbation for every thing, and condemnation for nothing. It recognizes no merit, no demerit, in human souls; no *special heaven* for pretended self-righteousness, and no special hell for a bleeding, suffering humanity. It accepts every creed, belief, and doctrine, every action, good and "bad," as being the lawful effect of a cause that lies in unseen spirit, which cause is above the power of human volition.

The thoughts herein written are gathered from practical life; from the kitchen and the parlor; from the garden and the barren field; from the workshop and the playhouse; from the gambling-house and the "house of God;" from the life of the poor man and the life of the rich man; from lives of want and lives of plenty; from lives of pleasure and lives of affliction; from the holy man's goodness and the wicked man's goodness; from those who condemn and those who bear condemnation; from the mountains and the valleys of human distinctions; from babyhood and from manhood; from the beauties and the deformities of nature; from the day and from the night; from the tempest and from the sunshine; from talking with devils and talking with angels; from earth, hell, and heaven; from tacit soul-persuasion; from a feeble development of intuition.

There is no starch of restraint to bind the freedom of the thoughts herein written; no schoolhouse training to polish them; no rhetorical order to systematize them; no church excellence to cover up their deformities; no fear of evil, devils, or men, of God, or angels, to cut short the utterance of a single word that the soul's persuasion dictates.

Many will say that this book is at fault in the correct use of words, and in the systematic arrangement of ideas. In the parlance of earthly logic, I must admit this to be true; but about it I have little concern. I have used words in keeping with my very imperfect earthly education, that were most convenient to express ideas, and have written down these ideas as they were spontaneously produced.

Unuttered thoughts always exist in our bosoms, and they are without order, without system; they are spontaneous. Our thoughts expressed in social and in business conversation abruptly change, regardless of system or of order. And wherein should there be order, system, and arrangement in a book, more than in spontaneous thought? I know not, and have made this book according to my knowledge.

Some repetition of ideas, in different forms of expression, is here allowed, for the purpose of making this doctrine more clearly understood.

The ground is unreservedly taken, that the influences of the material world are entirely negative to the spiritual world; that the spirit produces matter, and matter cannot affect that which produces it. The soul produces deeds that are called good and bad—beliefs that war with each other, that change and pass away—and by these products of the soul, it can in no way be influenced, retarded, or advanced, in its eternal progression.

The whole book is a very imperfect presentation of a doctrine—if a doctrine it may be called—that is ineffably beautiful, and unutterably grand; viz., the doctrine that *all existence is as it was meant to be by*

Infinite Wisdom; all that is, is good; all that is, is right.

Perfect faith in God is perfect confidence that all his works are good, the fruition of which is the kingdom of heaven in the soul, the millennium of peace on the earth.

CONTENTS.

Page.

GOOD AND EVIL, ... 1

QUESTIONS AND ANSWERS, ... 3

What is Nature? 3

What is God? 3

What is the Word of God? 4

What is the Bible of the Soul? 4

What is Religion? 5

What is Prayer? 5

What is Virtue? 5

What is Vice? 6

What is the Human Soul? 6

What is Belief? 7

What is the Human Body? 7

What is Death? 8

What is Suicide? 8

What is Life? 9

What is Intuition? 9

What is Human Reason? 9

What is Infidelity? 10

What are Human Distinctions? 10

What is Humanity? 10

What is Hell? 11

Page.
Where is Hell? ... 11
What is Heaven? ... 11
Where is Heaven? ... 12
How do we get to Heaven? ... 12
Are we in Hell or in Heaven? ... 12
What is Christ? ... 14
Who are the Followers of Christ? ... 14
How do we become Followers of Christ? ... 15
What feeds the Soul? ... 15
Can the Soul be injured? ... 16
Can the Soul retrogress? ... 16
What is the Soul's Immortality? ... 16
What is a Step in Progression? ... 17
How is Truth developed in the Soul? ... 17
Is there a Standard of Truth? ... 17
Can a Man make his Belief? ... 17
What is a Lie? ... 18
Is Public Opinion right? ... 18
What is Imagination? ... 18
Who loves not God? ... 18
What is Prostitution? ... 19
What are Wicked Men? ... 19
What are Great Men? ... 20
What Form of Religion is best? ... 20
Is one Man superior to another Man? ... 21
Is one Soul superior to another? ... 22
Who will oppose the Truth that declares every thing Right? ... 22
Who will denounce this Book? ... 22
What will the Sectarian Press say about this Book? ... 23

Page.
What Creed does this Book accept?.......................... 23
How can that be Right which seemeth Wrong? 24
Does Impurity exist in the Soul? 24
Do we make our Thoughts?................................... 24
Can the Soul forget? 25
If every thing is Right why should we make Efforts in Goodness?. 25
What is a Miracle?... 25
What is Association?....................................... 26
What will sustain the All-Right Doctrine? 26
What is Evil?.. 27
What is Good? 27
Can the Laws of Nature be broken?.......................... 27
What will disarm the Antagonism of Opposition?............. 27
What will be the principal Objection made to this Book? 28
What Condition of Soul will make our Heaven?............... 28
How broad is the Platform of the All-Right Belief?......... 28
What Condition of Soul will see that Whatever is, is Right?.... 28
Is the Doctrine of this Book new to this Age?.............. 29
Can one Soul produce a New Doctrine?....................... 29
For what are Human Reforms?................................ 30
For what are Written Commandments?......................... 30
Do Precepts and Rules of Action influence the Soul?........ 30
What is the Cure of what is called Evil?................... 31
Is it wrong to Curse and Swear?............................ 31
Does Imprisonment affect the Soul of the Prisoner?......... 31
May we Work Sundays?....................................... 32
What is Spiritualism?...................................... 33
How much is a Man's Reputation worth?...................... 34
Who are Mediums? 34

Page.
Which is the Way that leads to Heaven? 35
Is it Murder to hang a Man? 35
Is it Murder to kill a Man in War? 36
Is Ignorance the Cause of Suffering? 36
Is Ignorance the Cause of what we call Sin? 36
What makes Suffering and Sin? 36
What are Spiritual Manifestations? 37
Who are Dangerous Men? 37
What shall destroy the Fear of Death? 37
Will the All-Right Doctrine increase Immorality and Crime? ... 37
TRUTH 39
THE PURSUITS OF HAPPINESS 43
NATURE 50
NATURE RULES 53
WHAT APPEARS TO BE EVIL IS NOT EVIL 57
A SPIRITUAL COMMUNICATION 60
CAUSES OF WHAT WE CALL EVIL 63
EVIL DOES NOT EXIST 67
UNHAPPINESS IS NECESSARY 70
HARMONY AND INHARMONY 76
THE SOUL'S PROGRESS 79
INTUITION 84
RELIGION—WHAT IS IT? 88
SPIRITUALISM 97
THE SOUL ONLY IS REAL 106
SELF-RIGHTEOUSNESS 108
SELF-EXCELLENCE 111
VISION OF MRS. ADAMS 114
HUMAN DISTINCTIONS 115

Page.

EXTREMES ARE BALANCED BY EXTREMES............ 119

THE TIES OF SYMPATHY................................ 123

ALL MEN ARE IMMORTAL............................... 125

THERE ARE NO EVIL SPIRITS........................... 129

HARMONY OF SOUL THAT THE ALL-RIGHT DOCTRINE PRODUCES.. 133

OBSESSION... 141

OPINIONS OF OTHERS, AND REMARKS.................. 145

THE VIEWS OF THIS BOOK ARE IN PERFECT HARMONY WITH THE SAYINGS AND PRECEPTS OF CHRIST... 209

WHAT EFFECT DOES THE DOCTRINE, WHATEVER IS, IS RIGHT, HAVE UPON MEN AND SOCIETY?........ 216

WHATEVER IS, IS RIGHT.

GOOD AND EVIL.

"There surely is some guiding power
That rightly suffers wrong,
Gives vice to bloom its little hour,
But virtue late and long."

Good is eternal; evil is a phantom of time. Good is real and indestructible; evil is unreal and exists only as a shadow of matter; a shadow of creation made by the sunlight of Infinite Wisdom. We have been taught that some of the actions of human life are good, and others are evil; those that lead us to happiness are good, and those that lead us to suffering are evil. This recognition of evil has existed through all ages of the world to the present time.

In this view of life, which takes cognizance of evil, we have not recognized the fact that suffering is a lawful property of our earthly existence as much as happiness is; and that those acts that have caused suffering have been the effect of an unseen force of sufficient power to produce them, which force is *not* apparently, but *is really*, above human volition, and is in the ordering of Infinite Wisdom; is meant to be as it is.

For every deed of human life, there has been a cause sufficient to produce the deed, whether the deed has been called good or evil; and every cause and every effect exists in the bosom of Nature — is under the immediate and perfect government of Nature's laws. Every law of Nature is a law of God, every jot and tittle of which must be fulfilled. God being infinite, there can be no nature or law outside of infinitude. God being good, all that is in God is good. So every deed of human life is good — not one is evil.

Good is every thing that exists; it is the whole picture of life. Evil is the shading of the beautiful picture, existing only in material life; and so evil, in the picture, necessarily, is good.

QUESTIONS AND ANSWERS.

"—— I never tire
In questioning, but, at each response,
I find a depth from which I shrink.
My soul draws back and questions still."

What is Nature?

Nature is all space and all matter — all, a million times told, that our feeble consciousness can yet grasp; all life, and the manifestations of life; all that has passed, all that is, and all that ever will be. Nature, we conceive, is the manifestation of Infinite Power, Infinite Wisdom, and Infinite Perfection; it is the product of undefined harmony and unutterable beauty.

What is God?

All that we know of God is made manifest to us in nature. Beyond this we know nothing of God. We say that God is infinite in power, in wisdom, in presence, in love, in goodness. In every thing we may recognize the spirit of God, and in the nature of all things we have a limited sense of what God is. There is no place, no space, no thing, where God is not. There is no power that is not God's power; no condition that is not God's condition; no presence that is not God's presence; no love that is not God's love; no goodness that is not God's goodness. Evil has no place in God, so it must be nowhere.

What is the Word of God?

All matter, and what is called space, are pregnant with the word of God. An infinitude of worlds revolving in harmony, speak, in the awful grandeur of silence, the word of God to us. Unmeasured distance tells us of unreached realities. The uncounted sands, that lie beneath the unnumbered drops that make the mighty ocean, speak to us of Infinity. Unnumbered forms of life every moment breathe the word of God. The running brook, the waterfalls, the roaring waves, murmur the word of God. All the leaves on the forest trees — each one proclaims the word of God. The doleful wind sighs, the dashing tempest beats, the lightning flashes, and the thunder roars the word of God for us. Ten thousand songsters chant the word of God. Myriads of insects in varied notes proclaim the word of God. Each thing of life gives utterance to the word of God. In every human soul we read the word of God — always fresh, always new. We read the word of God on every leaf of Nature's book, fresh before us, from the lowest strata of the earth to the highest condition of angel life; in every thing that hath life we read the word of God, and in every thing that yet sleepeth in inanimate beauty, we may also read the word of God.

What is the Bible of the Soul?

We will call the great volume of Nature our Bible, in which we find the record that we call the word of God. On every gigantic leaf of Nature's book, God's own finger has written in indelible lines, every word of which is unalterable truth. This is the Bible of the soul of man; the Bible in which we may read, mark, learn, and inwardly digest the imperishable truths of God's infinite love.

My soul is my Bible, in which I read the truths of eternal life. My soul's longings and its desires are the utterances of my Bible that commands the food that satisfies its longings and its desires.

What is Religion?

Religion is the natural desire of the soul; a desire for something that the soul does not possess. Every desire is religion to the soul that produces the desire. Desire is a wish, a longing for something not yet possessed. Whatever the desire may be, whether it is called good or bad, that desire is the natural religion of the soul that develops the desire. Religion is natural and inevitable; it is a property of human life. Nature governs and directs it; the soul produces it.

What is Prayer?

Prayer is an uttered or unuttered petition to command what the soul craves. So near is prayer allied to religion, that they are inseparable. Every breath is a prayer; every throb of the heart is a prayer; every desire that makes every action of life is a prayer. Prayer, in every human soul, ceases not from the cradle to the grave. Nature commands us to pray without ceasing, and sternly enforces obedience. Christ also says, "Pray without ceasing." This we all do, and ever have done.

What is Virtue?

Virtue, we say, is self-denial; it is that manifestation of life which makes us happy; that contributes to our earthly well-being; that avoids pain and embraces pleasure; that shuns deformity and seeks beauty. Virtue is the angel guardian of material beauty; the mother of earthly happiness; the safeguard and the protector of the material garment that covers the soul while it lives on earth. Virtue, to our earthly existence, is beautiful; it is lovely. When earthly love ceases to exist, virtue ceases to exist, and in its place comes a higher development of soul.

What is Vice?

Vice is an enemy to this world's beauty. It is a manifestation of life that produces pain, and repels earthly love; it is sand-paper to the earthly covering of the soul, that takes all the earthly polish off, and some of the earthly substance too. It is an agent to break by degrees our earthly love. It wears off the material garments that clothe our souls in our earthly existence, and, by its agency, the soul gets freed from earthy matter sooner. Vice and virtue, too, are beautiful to the eyes of the soul. Both are right and in place.

What is the Human Soul?

An unmeasured and undefined reality; for aught we know it has no beginning, and we have a tacit consciousness that it has no end. It has reality above all conscious existence; it possesses inherent power over matter, and all the influences of the material world. We conceive that it emanates from Infinite Wisdom, and will ever and forever advance in its progression toward Infinite Perfectness. It is invisible to sensuous eyes, and cannot be judged of by sensuous comparisons. It cannot be influenced by things of earth or time. It is indestructible, and consequently, it cannot be injured; it is eternal, and consequently, cannot be influenced by that which is not eternal; it holds within itself the elements of all truth, and consequently, cannot be taught. Truth is developed in the soul by natural growth; so it can never receive a truth from the teachings of another soul. Every deed of human life is the effect of the soul; so good deeds or bad deeds can have no influence upon it. The soul is above the influence of all earthly powers; so by them it cannot be advanced or retarded in its progression. The human soul is the only significant possession of our existence. It is the alpha and the omega, the sum and substance of human life.

What is Belief?

Belief is a deduction of material philosophy; of earthly intelligence — that changes as material things change. It is of the evidences of material things, which, like footprints on the shores of time, are washed away and gone forever by one wave from the great ocean of spiritual truth that breaks through the porthole of the soul's intuition. Belief is a product of the soul in material existence, and like material things, is subject to change and dissolution. Belief is a property of the material world; it is worthless and meaningless to the spirit.

What is the Human Body?

It is the effect of the soul; it is the product of the soul's development; it is the effect of the soul's growth; it is a garment the soul is clothed with, and wears for a time. From the moment of its development the process of the soul's growth is ever struggling to throw it off. From the moment of its creation, its decay begins. The human body becomes in time the offal of the soul; it holds to the soul a while, but in the order of nature it must sooner or later fall off. While matter is held by the soul, life is manifest through it; the soul's life exists the same when matter leaves it as it did before; the soul is the same precisely after the garment is shed as it was before. Death of the human body has no influence upon the soul. The human body dies and returns to dust, and by this incident in the soul's existence, only the body changes — not the soul.

What is Death?

To life there is no death. Life can never die. All life inevitably lives forever. Life is spirit that produces matter that clothes life; which matter, when ripened and matured, falls from the thing of life like leaves that fall from the living tree. What we call death is but the falling off of the flesh, blood, and bones from the beautiful spirit of enduring life.

What is Suicide?

"Premature death," we say. In nature there is nothing too early — nothing too late — nothing is premature. From the moment of our birth to the period we call death, the hand of nature, acting through each one of us, is ever doing a suicidal work. Nature moves the murderer's hand no less than she prolongs life to ripened maturity. Suicide is only a separation of the material body from the soul before the threads are worn and rotten. The natural love of life generally avoids the necessity of this act, and when this natural love ceases to act, Nature takes her course, and what we call suicide is the consequence.

What is Life?

Life is spirit. Spirit is a property of eternity; all life, both vegetable and animal, we conceive is immortal. No life can ever cease to be. Life makes matter appear animated when in it, and when it goes out again matter appears dead. All we know of life is its manifestations through materialism, which afford us but a faint knowledge of its reality. What is life? It is impossible to tell by the aid of material philosophy; intuition, without the aid of words alone, can answer. Life is spirit, and spirit is immortality; and immortality is life — is spirit.

What is Intuition?

Intuition is spontaneous thought, developed by natural growth of soul, independent of all external influences; it is the tacit persuasion of the inner being; it is the positive knowledge of the soul that comes from whence we know not. It is the volition of truth; it is the light of spiritual realities; it is the bright and morning star that is rising in the spiritual firmament now; it is the monitor of the soul, and by it the soul learns its first lessons of eternal truth, and through eternity shall never cease to learn.

What is Human Reason?

It is one of the guardian angels of our material existence; it is the product of the soul acting through matter; it can control material things, not spiritual things; it is an effect of the soul that is allied to material philosophy, and with the material things of earth will sometime give place to the higher development of intuition.

What is Infidelity?

Infidelity is to me that which another believes, and that which I do not believe. If I believe in one creed only, I am infidel to all other creeds; if I believe in two creeds, I am less infidel; if I believe in all creeds I am not infidel at all. So the greatest infidel believes that only one creed is right, while he that is not an infidel at all, believes that every creed is right;—believes that every creed is an effect of a lawful cause that exists in nature.

What are Human Distinctions?

Properties of the material world that death brings to one level. Distinctions among men are changeable, unenduring; are of transient significance, which the laws of God in nature govern with impartiality, and reduce to one common dissolution—ashes to ashes, dust to dust. High and low are properties of matter, not of the soul; good and bad are distinctions of time, not of eternity; inferior and superior belong to earth, not to heaven.

What is Humanity?

Humanity is a great level sea of throbbing life, composed of countless millions of immortal souls germinating in the darkness of matter, to grow up in the light of spirit and blossom in heaven; one great household of beings, whose aims and purposes are one, viz., happiness now and happiness hereafter. Humanity is a family; God is the Father of this family; Nature takes care of this family, and holds every one sternly obedient to her laws, without any respect of persons — without any recognition of the distinctions of good and evil.

What is Hell?

Hell is suffering. Its conditions are contention and war; a conflict and a struggle for happiness; a desperate fight with the dark phantom called Evil; an unmitigated war with the shadow of matter called the Devil, who was never yet seen with sensuous eyes or with spiritual eyes. Hell is a soul-conflict, which is the effect of soul growth; it is a struggle between the material and the spiritual world; it is a breaking of earthly affections, and a rising of the soul out of the darkness of the material, to the light and beauty of spiritual life.

Where is Hell?

In the bosom of the sufferer, always. It may be anywhere, it may be everywhere, where suffering is. There is no avenue of earth where suffering does not exist.

What is Heaven?

Heaven is rest of the soul. All that is peace, harmony, joy, happiness, is heaven; all that presents evidence of right and good; all that evinces wisdom, order, design in the plan of creation, are emanations of beauty that make up the atmosphere of heaven, which every soul in heaven breathes. Heaven is a condition of the inner man, that sees goodness and right in every thing; order, design, harmony, and beauty existing in all places and conditions throughout the universe of God. Heaven is that condition of soul which feels that *whatever is, is right.*

Where is Heaven?

Christ has said that "the kingdom of heaven is within us." There is no place to look for heaven, except it be within the longing, throbbing soul. If anywhere, there heaven is, and each soul for itself finds it there. Heaven is everywhere, is anywhere where the soul is in peace, in harmony, and in love with all existence.

How do we get to Heaven?

By the natural process of soul-development; by suffering and conflict; by the power of the laws of God acting in nature. Never by our own efforts.

Are we in Heaven or Hell?

Do we desire to know what our own condition is — how much we possess of heaven, and how much of hell? Let us examine ourselves. Heaven is *peace*, and hell is *war*. How much wrong do we find in the world? Our opposition, our warlike faculties are active in proportion to our discovery of wrong, and our heaven is commensurate with our peace; harmony in the soul with all things. A heavenly condition of the soul does not see or resist any wrong. Is our condemnation sent forth to every thing, and everybody?

Are people all to blame — all very wicked — and is almost every thing wrong? If so, we are in that condition of spiritual growth where the laws of nature are throwing off the elements of wrong in us. This is a necessity in one degree of the soul's growth, which degree is war, antagonism, inharmony, is hell.

"Seek first the kingdom of heaven," says the holy Jesus. By our natural growth we will find it. Have we grown to it? How near are we allied to that heavenly condition, where all is peace, harmony, and love; where all that exists appears right, and nothing that exists appears wrong?

A soul of heaven has confidence in God; in all his works; sees no wrong anywhere; sees beauty in every thing; sees God in all nature; unmeasured beauty in the immortal soul; beauty in deformity the same as in symmetry — for the hand of God is in both; sees through the flimsy vapor of pollution and degradation emanating from one soul, as being only the result of a purifying process of that soul; the lawful effect of a means our Father uses to bring his child to heaven sooner. The soul of heaven sees unutterable beauty in immortal life, whatever may be its condition of progress, or degree of growth. All God's children are beautiful; all life and all things are beautiful. The soul of heaven is in harmony with the lowest life, with even the elements of a stone; there is no repulsion; can be with serpents without a shudder or a shriek, and see in them the work of a divine hand; can behold the worst manifestations of human life without reproach or blame. Are we at peace with all men and all life? Do we see no wrong, but every thing right? If so, there is peace within the soul; the kingdom of heaven is there, and the soul is nearly allied in condition to that world where all is peace, harmony, and love — where there is no evil, no fault, no wrong.

Thus we may measure our capacities for hell or heaven — for an early or a more advanced condition of spirit-life. Our attractions *for* evil are determined by our perceptions *of* evil — our attractions *for* good, by our perceptions *of* good.

Then are we in hell or in heaven? Each one can answer for himself or for herself by looking into his or her own heart.

What is Christ?

A brilliancy of light is presented now to my vision, too great for the present feeble development of my soul to endure! I cannot tell. I cannot define the immense magnitude of eternal beauty that lies before me! I fail to tell who Christ is! In the deepest humility I can only ask for strength to sustain me, and for shadows to darken my vision!

What is Christ? I do not wonder now that humanity called Christ, God. In tearful admiration — in shrinking awe — I can only ask is Christ our example? Are we to be what he is? If so, O God! sustain and guide us in our progression.

Who are the Followers of Christ?

Those who drink the cup of bitterness to its dregs; those who suffer in the gardens of earth; those whose earthly existence is crucified; those who bind up the bleeding wounds of a suffering humanity; those who eat with publicans and sinners; those who commune with devils and with angels; those whose affections are set on spiritual things that endure, more than on things of earth that perish; those who recognize a power that transcends the boundaries of matter, and reaches out to grasp the limitless beauties that are prepared and waiting for them in the many mansions of their heavenly homes.

How do we become Followers of Christ?

By natural soul-development, not by preaching, praying, singing, exhortation, talking, or writing. We become followers of Christ involuntarily, by the inflowing of God's holy love that feeds the soul and makes it grow, independent of volition, or all the material constructions or appliances in church organizations, rites, forms, and ceremonies. He who professes to war with the inflexible powers of nature, and with the soul opinions of the masses of humanity, because he is a member of a church, and thinks evil is everywhere outside, is no more a follower of Christ than he who is outside the church.

What feeds the Soul?

That which is like itself; that which is unseen, immortal, and eternal. Nothing that belongs to earth can feed it, or influence its progression. The soul is fed by the unseen rivers of God's love that flows everywhere. The soul is fed and nurtured for a while in unconsciousness, as the material existence of an infant is, for a while, fed and nurtured in unconscious development in the arms of a fond and loving parent. That which feeds the soul and makes it grow, is beyond our powers of development yet to understand and know.

Can the Soul be injured?

If the soul can be injured, it must show marks, when injured, of decay and dissolution, thus rendering the certainty of its immortality, at best, precarious. To injure the soul is to take worth from its value, and repeated injuries would render it valueless. This cannot be done to that which has eternal worth. The soul is life; life cannot be injured. Susceptibility of the soul to injury, contradicts its property of immortality. The soul cannot be injured.

Can the Soul retrogress?

If the soul can retrogress it does not possess the property of eternal progress, for repeated retrogressions would carry it back where its identity commenced, and thus its identity would be lost, whereby its progress would be annihilated. The soul can neither go backward, nor be retarded, for its inherent powers of eternal progress command an influence that holds it and moves it onward forever.

What is the Soul's Immortality?

It is a problem of human existence, unsolved by human philosophies. The soul's immortality has never been proved by the philosophies of matter, and never can be. The soul's immortality is a reality which becomes positive to our consciousness *alone* by our own intuition. Intuition is the only real evidence of immortality. The communion of spirits with mortals is a material evidence that the soul lives after death, as positive and as sure as any evidence of material philosophy; but there is a higher and more abiding evidence of the soul's immortality than this, which is the spontaneous persuasion of every soul.

What is a Step in Progression.

It is an intuitive, conscious perception of a new truth that nature has developed out of the soul. Every step of progress is a step on ground untrodden by the soul that takes it. Every step in progress is an original experience of truth, to the soul that develops it.

How is Truth developed in the Soul?

By intuition, always. The soul never did, nor never can, receive that which to itself is a truth, from external teachings — from the schoolhouse or the meeting-house. The first truth that the soul ever received, which is to be a property of its eternal existence, is the effect of intuitive development.

Is there a Standard for Truth?

Yes. Each soul has its own standard; but no one can see a truth for another. Each soul is alone the lawful producer and possessor of its own truths. There is no universal standard of religious truth yet recognized for every one, because we see yet with sensuous vision, only one or more sides of a thing that has a thousand other sides. A spirit view, perhaps, will cover the whole, and see every side as parts of one great, beautiful, harmonious whole. To intuitive perception there may be a universal standard of truth.

Can a Man make his Belief?

No; no more than he can make the laws of nature

that produced himself. Belief is an effect of life, moulded in our natural organization, by which it is produced. Belief is as involuntary as the beating of the heart; as is our inspiration and expiration; as is our birth and our death.

What is a Lie?

A lie is true to the cause that produced it; so what we call a lie is a truth that exists in nature, just as real as is what we call a truth. The cause of a lie exists in nature; the cause of a truth exists in nature, and the effect of each cause is wrought out in nature. Nature is always true in her work; so both a truth and what we call a lie are lawful and right in the great plan of existence. A lie is a truth intrinsically; it holds a lawful place in creation; it is a necessity.

Is Public Opinion right?

It is always right, for it is a lawful effect of a natural cause. Thus every opinion is right. Public opinion is always right for that condition of the public mind that produces and supports it.

What is the Imagination?

The faint and feeble glimmerings of approaching intuition, more real than earthly science and earthly philosophies; more real and more enduring than the monuments of time which brick and mortar make.

Who Loves not God?

No one. Every one loves something, and in every thing exists the spirit of God. In every love exists our love of God; and every one loves to the full extent of his or her capacity. Love is never the effect of volition; but is always spontaneous. Every one naturally loves something, and every love that exists in the universe, no matter what that love is, is a love which the lover has for God. Everybody loves God.

What is Prostitution?

It is a condition of earthly degradation, produced by the distinctions of the material world, not by soul comparisons. The degradation of prostitution is a phantom of materialism that belongs to self-righteousness; that is produced by the fictitious distinctions of self-excellence; prostitution, so-called, in reality is an *undisguised* condition of life; an open expression of the elements of existence that are spontaneous and natural, and that are antagonistic to material glory. Prostitution is an enemy to the good, the true, the beautiful— that are the crowning excellencies of the material world.

What are Wicked Men?

Those whose works make themselves suffer, and those who are around them. Wicked men are distinguished from holy men by the exhibition of their outer life; by manifestation of their souls through materialism. The standard of judgment that defines a wicked man, is material, and, consequently, must be uncertain; the vision that sees a wicked man, is sensuous, consequently must fail to see realities that are unchangeable. What are called wicked deeds are lawful effects of one soul, as much as what are called holy deeds are lawful effects of another soul. There is a cause that lies back, beyond the power of volition in the holy man, and in the wicked man; both are perfectly controlled by the laws of nature. The garment of material love, that the soul of the wicked man wears, becomes broken, torn, and ragged; the garment of material love, that the soul of the holy man wears, is more perfect, is whole and beautiful. It is material love in perfectness that constitutes what is called holiness; it is material love that is broken and torn, that constitutes what we call wickedness. Both holiness and wickedness are lawful in nature, and *are each unqualifiedly right.* One supports our earthly affections, the other breaks them; one holds the soul in bondage longer, the other lets it free sooner.

What are Great Men?

Greatness among men is alone a property of the sensuous world; it does not belong to the world of spirits. Greatness of mind belongs to the philosophies of the earth, which philosophies, like the earth, are material, and are subject to the same laws. No greatness among men goes beyond the boundaries of the love of earth. The right that we have, to claim that the spirits of Washington, Fenelon, Shakspeare, and Napoleon, are a whit greater than the spirits of their washerwomen and scavengers, is only warranted by the standard of material philosophy, which, to the soul, is as a fiction; is as a shadow of matter.

What form of Religion is best?

The religion of the Indian is as true to the Indian, as the religion of the Christian is true to the Christian. So it is of all the various religions on earth. The religion of Mahomet is no more true than the religion of Christ. Each is true to the cause that produces it; both are the effect of soul causes, of human action; both are lawful—each one is in its time and place. So it is of all religious sects and creeds. Every sect is right, every creed right. Every form of religion is best to the condition that produces it.

Is one Man superior to another Man?

In his physical being he may be. He may weigh more; he may have more money; he may have more of the philosophies of matter; he may have handsomer morals and a cleaner earthly religion; he may have a handsomer face and form, a handsomer dress; he may cheat more legally and trade more shrewdly; he may talk more fluently and write more elegantly; he may live in a handsomer house and repose more comfortably in the arms of luxury. In all these earthly things, and a thousand more of a kindred nature, one man may be superior to another; but all this superiority is like the superiority seen in the

——"track of feet,
Left on Tampa's desert strand;
Soon as the rising tide shall beat,
Their marks shall vanish from the sand."

The soul of one man is not superior to the soul of another man, for if one possesses the properties of eternal life and unending progress, the other also does. These properties, when recognized, put an end to the thought of superior and inferior, as applied to the beautiful soul. Hence one man is not superior to another man.

Is one Soul superior to another Soul?

In spiritual realities there can be no comparisons; comparisons are forbidden; there is no superiority, no inferiority. Comparison belongs to the material world; judgment does not reach the spiritual world, where the shadows of matter have vanished. Each soul has unmeasured beauties, unmeasured progress, and a oneness of harmony, a blending of sympathy, that obliterates the lines of comparison whereby judgment ceases to exist. One soul is not superior to another soul. The soul in spirit alone can obey the command, "*Judge not,*" for judgment belongeth not to the soul.

Who will oppose the Truth that declares every thing right?

Those who are yet unable to bear the immense beauty of its mighty reality. The bright and dazzling effulgence, the clear and beautiful light of this truth, has been wisely hidden from our feeble vision for a time, by a belief in the existence of evil, which in the light of truth is only a shadow — a shadow of necessity — which is a fiction in reality. Sensuous, limited perception, will oppose this beautiful truth, until the vision is strong enough to bear it.

Who will denounce this Book?

Earthly science; popular religion; self-excellence and self-righteousness. Men who have gathered in considerable knowledge of the philosophies of matter; who are very correct, consistent, and conservative; very statistical, historical, elaborate, and argumentative —if *they* condescend to read it, will say this book is wofully wanting in that which they love and cherish most. Men who are bound to the bigotry of a single creed will say it is infidelity, because they cannot believe any thing outside their own creed; consequently, what they cannot believe is to them infidelity, and will be branded with their own stamp of ignominy. Self-excellent and self-righteous men will say in their hearts, "Why, this book brings all men upon one common level; if no one is better, if no one is worse, all have equal claims to happiness. Where is my reward for my excellence and my righteousness above the man who is not so excellent and so righteous as I am?" To such this book will give offence, and from such it will receive unmeasured scandal. But such treatment of views not contained in their own creeds is perfectly right, for it is lawful in nature.

What will the Sectarian Press say about this Book?

I suppose sectarian editors will hold this book with the tongs, turn its leaves over with the poker, and speak of it as being as fatal to their religion and morals as *the sirocco*, *the upas*, and *the serpent's venom* is to human life. If sectarian newspapers notice this book at all, it will be presented in the light of *only one creed*, and will be condemned with severity. This will be right.

What Creed does this Book accept?

Every creed — not one more than another. Every creed is true in its condition and right in its place. This doctrine of "Whatever Is, is Right," takes in every creed and every doctrine; it has no narrow limits of belief; no boundaries of sect; no landmarks of religion, but it reaches out to the shores of spiritual infinity. This doctrine opposes no creed nor any belief in creation.

How can that be Right which seemeth Wrong?

The right lies latent in what is called the wrong. The most beautiful things come to us sometimes shrouded in a mantle of darkness, and it is this darkness that we call wrong. Out of the darkest cloud comes the intensest light — the lightning's flash; out of the dark night comes the gentle dews to refresh the earth; out of stagnant, muddy water comes the loveliest, sweetest flower; out of affliction comes a softening and purification of our lives; out of wrong actions comes chastisement that humbles and beautifies our existence; out of what seems to us the greatest wrongs comes always the greatest good.

Does Impurity exist in the Soul?

No. Impurity exists only in matter and is only palpable to material perception. To the soul, and to the vision of the soul all things are pure — thus we say, to the pure in heart all things are pure. Sensuous eyes see impurity in sensuous things. Soul perception discovers no impurity anywhere in the creation of God.

Do we make our Thoughts?

Our thoughts are always involuntary. Like the beating of our hearts and like our respiration, they are not produced by our will. There must be some acting power behind, unseen by us, that makes us live and breathe and think. We neither make nor control our thoughts. All thoughts are right. Devilish thoughts have no less merit than angel thoughts. All thoughts are the spontaneous productions of nature.

Can the Soul forget?

Every truth of intuition is indelibly inscribed upon the soul, and will live there forever. The *seeming* truths of evil fade away and are forgotten in the light of *real* truths. Shadows vanish and light endures. A consciousness of evil is not intuition, and is not inscribed upon the soul; shadows of matter do not influence the soul; goodness springs forth in shadows; we remember the good forever, but the shadows fade away. Intuition comes up in the darkness of philosophies, as the sun comes up to dispel the darkness of the night.

If every thing is right, why should we make Efforts in Goodness?

Because we cannot help so doing. To do good is a part of the work of life — and to our earthly and spiritual consciousness it is the most beautiful part. To do that which makes ourselves and others happy is a natural necessity of our earthly existence, and of our spiritual existence. Do we ask why we should make efforts in goodness? The reason is, necessity; the cause is, the soul.

What is a Miracle?

That which human philosophy cannot explain. Every thing is a miracle to the present development of our consciousness. We have never seen nor comprehended the yet unseen causes of existence and the unseen laws that govern all things. The production of space is to us a miracle, for it is a secret; the production of life is a miracle, for it is to us a secret; the production of matter by spirit is a miracle, for it is a secret. We have no knowledge of the causes that produce, and of the laws that govern, all things, and they are miracles to us.

What is Association?

It is the effect of spirit attraction, which attraction makes like seek its like throughout the universe. In nature particles attract kindred particles, and on the threads of spirit attraction they run to meet each other, and their embrace makes physical forms, makes association of physical atoms. The earth is thus made and all its various parts; the granite rock and all rocks; the sands and grains produced by attrition again reform in solid masses. Trees are thus formed, all vegetables, and all animals. The human body is thus produced. It is spirit that produces all associations through the agency of unseen life. The association of intelligent beings is governed by the same law of spirit attraction.

What will sustain the All-Right Doctrine?

The teachings of Christ will sustain it. Common sense will sustain it. The soul's deepest longings will sustain it. The reign of peace will sustain it. Heaven will sustain it. Humanity will some time sustain it, and all the powers of hell will join their efforts with the angels of love and mercy and work for it, for in it exist the elements of a universal heaven, a heaven for all, without one single exception; a heaven from which no outcast ever goes.

What is Evil?

What is called evil is good. Nothing is evil in reality, for what appears on the surface to be evil, is only a necessary effect of goodness; it is the effect of wisdom acting ever, for the best good of all. Evil is an *ignis fatuus*, chased by all humanity, but was never yet grasped; it is a shadow of earthly vision that will never be seen in the existence of spiritual light.

What is Good?

Good is every thing, for every thing is good. Every thing that is, was produced by Infinite Wisdom and Infinite Goodness. The day is good, the night is good; light is good, and darkness is good; knowledge is good, and ignorance is good; virtue is good, and sin is good; happiness is good, and suffering is good; life is good, and death is good; every human being is good, and every human action is good; God is good, and every thing that he has made is good.

Can the Laws of Nature be broken?

No. If the laws of nature could be broken, they might be injured and destroyed. It is impossible to break, injure, influence, or destroy a law of nature. Every law of matter and of spirit is fixed and unalterable, and each in its own condition is always fulfilled.

What will disarm the Antagonism of Opposition?

A cessation of opposition; perfect harmony with all things that exist; perfect peace with God and with all men; in a word, a recognition that whatever is, is right, and what will be, will be right.

What will be the Principal Objection made to this Book?

It will be claimed that it is infidelity. In answer to this objection I would ask, In what is this book infidel? Does it not believe in every thing? It accepts every creed as being true to the cause that produced each. It accepts every word of the Bible as being true, and every word of every other book as being true also. It accepts every manifestation of human life as being a lawful effect of a cause in nature. This book "accepteth all things, believeth all things," and therefore it *is not* infidelity.

What Condition of Soul will make our Heaven?

That condition alone which can recognize a heaven gained for every other soul in existence; a condition that has shed the scales of self-righteousness and sees no evil in others; a condition that produces the deep soul conviction, and the clear spiritual perception, that whatever is, is right.

How broad is the Platform of the All-Right Belief?

As broad as the universe. It is a platform on which every creed and every belief has a place. Every religion that is called religion, and every religion that is not called religion, is within the circle of this religion. This platform is broad enough to take every thing and everybody upon it, and reject nothing and nobody. It is humanitarian and universal; on it, all the inhabitants of hell, earth, and heaven belong, with equal rights.

What Condition of Soul will see that Whatever is, is Right?

The condition of intuition alone which *feels* this

doctrine true, and with the vision of the soul can *see* it true. All external evidence, all the philosophies of the material world, can never solve the problem of evil, and prove and see that it is right. The condition of the soul that sees goodness in every thing, sees above the uncertain evidences of the philosophies of time and matter.

Is the Doctrine of this Book new to this Age?

The recognition that whatever is, is right, is not new. But the doctrine that the soul cannot be influenced by the powers of the material world, by human actions and teachings, by any deed, or any earthly manifestation of life, to this age and generation, *is a new doctrine.* This doctrine is intuitively developed in the unspoken feelings of thousands to-day. Tacit persuasion expresses it in spirit.

The consciousness of the truth that the soul can only be influenced by that which is like itself, that which is unseen and immortal, is the effect of intuition, not the effect of education, for no books and no human teachings tell us this. The doctrine, of whatever is, is right, in this view of the soul's relation to the material world, alone can be accepted. The philosophies of the earth can never accept this doctrine. That power of the soul which can see spirit causes, the power of intuition alone, can or will accept the doctrine of whatever is, is right. This age develops the recognition of intuition, as being a thing more real than reason and philosophy.

Can one Soul produce a new Doctrine?

No. A new doctrine or a new thought is the product of an age, not of an individual. Humanity by an unseen power of sympathy develops truth, and it finds utterance through many simultaneously. All humanity help to produce the development of a new truth, of a new invention.

For what are Human Reforms?

For the advancement of the excellencies of the material world; all reformatory steps are the effects of the growing soul, *never* a means of the soul's growth. Temperance societies, anti-slavery societies, anti-tobacco societies, moral and intellectual culture societies, and all religious societies, alone tend to material excellence and advance material glory. One *good, well-managed, popular, anti-self-righteous society* would break the backbone of them all. But all these societies are the lawful effects of the expanding human soul, in its early infant growth. As effects of the soul they are necessary and right. Not one of them has any influence upon the soul's progress.

For what are Written Commandments?

For government and order in the material world. No commandment either written or spoken, ever yet had any influence upon the soul.

Do Precepts and Rules of Action influence the Soul?

Never; in no possible contingency; for the soul is above the influence of language made of words. Precepts and rules of action are for the material, not the spiritual, world.

What is the Cure of what is called Evil?

In answer to this question, I would ask, first, is nature sick? Does nature need any remedial agents? We talk of curing evil. Why, do we know that to talk thus, is to talk about curing God. Does Infinite Power need a cure? If so, for what? For the manifestations of Infinite Wisdom in the order of creation, which the feeble perception of man cannot see the purpose of? No; we can suggest no cure for the benefit of the already perfect order of Infinite Wisdom and Power as manifested through all nature.

Is it wrong to curse and swear.

Men curse and swear; and, for aught we know, they have since Eve gave birth to Cain. There is a cause for this; and while this cause exists, men will curse and swear. Acid water mixed with soda water has always made bubbles rise on the surface, and always will; for this there is a cause, too, over which man has no control; man cannot curse and swear without a cause; bubbles will not rise on water without a cause.

Nature calls forth the true elements of every soul, not unlawfully, but lawfully. Has any one a good reason for saying that the cause in nature that makes men swear, is not right? We may say that cursing and swearing is very foolish, but we cannot say the cause is outside of nature.

Does Imprisonment affect the Soul of the Prisoner?

No. Prison-houses answer one end of human law. We may confine within a prison, a man's material existence, while all the powers of earth cannot there confine his soul. No human tribunal, no prison walls, nor iron bars, can confine the soul's thoughts and desires. The *thoughts* of my brother, who is confined in the dungeon of a prison, are not confined there; they travel at their own pleasure; perhaps to the fireside of their earliest conscious existence, there to meet the embrace of a loving mother and affectionate sisters; they may travel through all the scenes of past life, and all over the earth, and, by the aid of angels, the thoughts of the so-called rebel may wing their flight to behold the beauties of the spiritual world, and then on, and on, toward limitless infinity. The soul cannot be touched or influenced by human laws, by prison discipline. Human legislations, human tribunals, and human executions, are effects of the soul — not things which can touch or influence it. All these are for the intended purpose of keeping the crockery in the warehouse of the material world from being smashed and broken; but the success is *almost* a failure, if not quite. I do not say that these things are wrong. No; they are right; they are just as lawful in Nature's courses, as are the crimes that cause their existence — all are effects of Nature's causes.

May we work on Sunday?

Sunday, we have been taught, is more holy than any other day. Does the revelation of God in nature say this? We breathe, and our hearts beat about the same on Sunday as on Monday; we eat and drink the same; vegetation grows the same; the earth revolves; water runs; the sun shines. All things in nature go on the same on Sunday as they do on the other days of the week. Is nature our Bible? If so, then we will go there to know what we shall do on Sunday. Christ was spontaneous and natural; he worked on Sunday, and taught us to, notwithstanding the Jewish law was against it. In all the vast domain of nature, there cannot be discovered any difference in her works on Sunday from her works on any other day of the week. The sacredness claimed for Sunday above any other day that God has made is a shadow which fades out in the light of common sense. It is nowhere found written in the Bible of nature.

Sunday may be a day of rest and recreation. And when we labor less to protect *self-possessions;* when we need no locks, no bolts to turn against our brothers; no landmarks and fences to tell what is "*mine,*" "*not yours;*" when we need no courts of justice to divide what property is mine and what is yours; when we need no guns to shoot men with — then we shall have to labor less, and we may have two days in the week of rest and recreation instead of one. And at our pleasure we may hold converse with one another and with angels; we may work, or we may play.

What is Spiritualism?

Ages yet to come will not define this word. The superficial fact that spirits do communicate, implies but a faint idea of the unmeasured reality that lies beneath this external, well-proven fact of its truth. Deep hidden yet lie the realities of Spiritualism; unmeasured, ungrasped, and undefined are the immortal beauties of the soul that the gateway of Spiritualism shall open to human consciousness.

How much is Reputation worth?

Reputation may be measured alone by the standard of material things.

Almost all public writers and speakers spend a great many words and a great deal of time to make a fair and handsome presentation of their own good character and excellent virtues. One-half that is said and written is to this end.

How much is the good opinion of a man worth to you? Take twelve and a half cents unjustly away from a man who holds you in the highest repute, and it balances his account with you. Good repute can be bought or sold for dollars, and generally for cents. Let a man once be aware that you infringe on his financial rights, and what is his estimate of your goodness worth? Nothing. Good repute does nothing for a man beyond dollars and cents, and very little there. How tenacious we are of *good repute*, and how lax we are of *real merit.* Reputation belongs to this world, not to the spiritual world. It is worth as much and no more than is any trash of matter to the spirit.

Who is a Medium?

Everybody that has a soul. Every human being is a medium, and every moment of earthly existence each one is under the immediate influence of spirits. All guardian spirits influence mortals through medium powers of their own.

"There is not a soul however sad and lowly, but has some angel wings clasped around its form, — wings of tenderness, whereon all its emanations of hope and love are impressed. Who is he that walks alone, that has no guardian wings about him, and never listens to their soft, sweet flutterings? Every soul has a guardian one, as truly as every body has its own rays of light, and its own breath of atmosphere. There is not an unguarded one in the universe. * * * *

Then think not, ye who are waiting and hoping for some celestial guardian to watch over you, that the earnest wish and desire will not be filled."

Every one, the "wickedest" and the holiest, has medium powers sufficient for his or her own demands for spirit truths. The guardianship of spirits over every child of earth indicates the medium powers of all.

Which is the Way that leads to Heaven?

There is no way in which the soul goes forth in life that does not lead directly to heaven.

> Not a single path on earth is trod,
> That does not lead the soul to God.

The wayward and the wise; the just and the unjust; the exalted and the lowly; the poor and the rich; the clean and the unclean; the intelligent and the ignorant; the rebel and the saint — each one goes in the way the soul directs, and every way points to heaven, and will lead us all home at last, after this wearisome journey of earthly life is ended.

Is it Murder to hang a Man?

Just as much as it is to cut a man's throat. And if there is blame and responsibility attached to cutting a man's throat, there is blame and responsibility attached to hanging a man. But to neither is blame or responsibility attached, for both are the effect of spirit, the product of Nature's laws. Every murder is lawful to that state of human life that produces the murder. Murder is murder at any time, and in any place, and murder can never be produced without the existing element of murder, which element is always the necessary cause of murder. Men who support murder on the gallows are murderers as much as is the midnight assassin.

Is it Murder to kill a Man in War?

Just as much murder to kill a man in war as it is to kill a man anywhere else, or in another way. To kill a man in one condition is murder just as much as it is to kill a man in any other condition. To take a man's life by force in one place, and in one condition, is murder just as much as it is to take a man's life by force in any other place and in any other condition. Men who go to, and support, war, are murderers, as much as a man is who kills another man in any condition.

Is Ignorance the Cause of Suffering?

No. He who suffers most often knows the most, and he who suffers least knows the least.

Is Ignorance the Cause of what we call Evil?

No. The wickedest are often the most intelligent, and the holiest the most ignorant.

What makes Suffering and Sin?

Infinite Wisdom.

What are Spiritual Manifestations?

Every manifestation of life in the body and out, is a manifestation of spirit.

Who are Dangerous Men?

The man who is developed to a practical acceptance of the all-right doctrine can be trusted in all things; the man who is not developed to the acceptance of this doctrine may be trusted in some things — not in all.

The men who see the most wrong in the world — if any dangerous men there be — are the most dangerous.

What shall destroy the Fear of Death?

The perception of the wisdom and power of God as manifested in every thing; the power to comprehend the truth that all things are made in *good*, for *good*, and by *good;* the perception of no wrong anywhere. In this condition the soul falls into the arms of death without fear, filled with unmeasured trust.

Will the Doctrine of All-Right increase Immorality and Crime?

No. Those who love and commit immorality and crime will not yet accept this doctrine; cannot accept it; and it is right to the condition of such that they should not. Those who can fully accept this doctrine have the power developed to see that every immoral and criminal act committed is as much to be avoided as steps taken on red-hot coals of fire. Every step taken in the direction of immorality and crime has always been a step taken in darkness and as fatal to happiness as steps taken with naked feet on burning coals. The intuition that develops the truth to human consciousness, that whatever is, is right, develops also the power to see the inseparable union of immoral and criminal deeds with suffering. Human nature never burns itself willingly. Impelled by an unseen power in darkness, it has often been burnt — and the burning has been necessary, has been for good. The development of the all-right doctrine inevitably and forever carries the soul above the commission of an immoral or a criminal act.

TRUTH.

Truth is law. Law is God. Truth is infinite, as God is. God fills all matter, all space, and all life. Truth does the same. Truth is everywhere; it has no rival, no antagonism. Truth is complete, supreme, and triumphant, being everywhere made manifest, in darkness, in light, working out sure and inevitable results. Truth is an inherent and unseen property of all things that exist in the universe of God.

The poor man and the rich man have equal claims to truth; the learned and the ignorant are equally its possessors; the wicked and the righteous, the foolish and the wise, each one and every one is decked, in spirit, with the unfading garlands of truth. Each fact of creation is a truth. The crude strata of the earth are as pregnant with truth as are the regions of blessed spirits; hell is as replete with truth as heaven is. Every thing, animate and inanimate, exists in truth, and is held by stern necessity, obedient to the laws of condition, by truth. Truth is no less partial to erring childhood than it is to the rectitude of mature manhood; it is as useful and as free to the infant as it is to the venerable old man. Truth is as constant to the condition of the liar as to the man of veracity; it is impartially given to both. It is given the same in high and low life; it is unalterable and fixed in all places and at all times. It is the law of God; it is sure always, and its power is commensurate with the power of Deity.

We talk of *true* life, and of a life that is *not true*. How can there be any life that is not true? Is not every thing that exists in the great world of mind and matter made by God, and ever and immediately under the government of his laws? Is there any thing without law, and are there any laws that are not God's laws? And so far as the feeble perception of man is able to reach out, is there any thing to be found that God has not made in wisdom, and also governs in wisdom? Has God created any thing except in truth? I can see truth in all nature; there is not one exception in any thing. What we call a lie, is to itself a truth; it is according to the law that produced it, and the law of a lie is a law of nature; it is a necessity of that condition of nature, that condition of darkness from which it had its birth. Then to that condition it is right, for it is an unalterable necessity, in its place. Darkness in the physical world is natural and necessary, and so it is in the mental and spiritual world, existing in matter, the same. So darkness is true in nature — is true in its place; it is truth as much as light is. The soul comes up through the physical world in darkness, and all that belongs to physical existence the soul must pass, and every thing that pertains thereto is true to its condition therein. These truths in nature we perceive not when existing in the conditions of darkness. There is a point to be gained in the soul's progress, from which it shall view, in the light of its own development, all the conflicts and darkness it has passed as having been necessary and right, in time and place — true, in the ordering of a wise Providence. The conflicts we meet in darkness seem to us evil; but could we see now, as we shall see sometime, with unclouded vision, the grand ultimate, the whole chain of cause and effect, the purposes, plans, and execution of Divine Wisdom, all life and its manifestations would be seen pregnant with truth, working out the highest good for all earth's children, without one single exception.

Truth is everywhere — in every thing. What we call false is only so because our darkened perceptions fail to discover the reality, which is truth; and it is no less truth because our visions that see it false are clouded. All nature is unalterably true; and all life and its manifestations is nature's life, and nature's manifestations. Groans and sighs, the recognition of evil, its resistance and condemnation; the consciousness of self-excellence, and the recognition of error and sin in humanity with the unmeasured consequences of sadness that follow; ten thousand beliefs and anti-beliefs that agitate the religious and moral world; misery and suffering, degradation and poverty, riches, prosperity, virtue, morals, and all the excellencies of the earth — all these are the legitimate offspring of nature; nature's law runs through the whole; this law is truth existing in every condition, and in all these varied manifestations.

There is no life, or effect of life, good or bad, high or low, that is not true to the condition from which it has its birth; that is not a part of the plan of God's creation, designed in wisdom and executed in love.

A belief in free moral agency is a natural product of a degree of the soul's growth; it is the inevitable effect of a certain condition of the soul-development; so is infidelity; and so it is of all the various religious creeds, dogmas, and opinions. A belief in fatalism and in destiny, is also an effect of the same. Bigotry and self-excellence are the effects of a natural cause — are the inevitable result of the soul in a certain condition of its onward and upward march of progress. All the crimes and wrong deeds of the earth are the manifestations of truth — are the inevitable effect of acting law, which law is nature's and which nature is God.

All these conditions of life that produce these various manifestations are conditions true to themselves, and are exactly in their time and place — are necessary and inevitable. And every soul, in some way, must pass, each to become conscious of the truths that belong to each, to see that all the falsities, as we say, of each are made so only by the weakness of our vision.

All hail that glorious day! when, with unclouded vision, humanity shall see every thing that now appears false and deformed, a truth of God, symmetrical and beautiful.

THE PURSUIT OF HAPPINESS.

"The pursuit of man is happiness," and, to gain it, "no man may put off the law of God."

Both of these passages are true; yet some may say, that most men are in the pursuit of unhappiness, and that God's laws may be and are put off.

My experience thus far in life has taught me that man pursues happiness at all times, in all places, and in all conditions; and all laws are God's laws; laws that may not be put off; they are inevitable, unchangeable, fixed, and certain.

This complex web of life is made up of all the avenues of happiness in which men naturally run, governed by the law of God—law which Christ came not to destroy, and has said that not one jot or tittle of it shall pass away till all be fulfilled.

Many and varied are the avenues of the soul of man in which he runs out to find happiness. In each he goes, as law directs, as the peculiar organization is developed out of the germ of eternal life planted in each, tends. The unerring law of God governs, and the nature of the spirit-germ points the way. God sowed the seed of human life and governs it by his laws. "God rules the destinies of men." No man rules or governs; yet he thinks he does. All the avenues of life in which the human soul wanders, in pursuit of happiness, tend to one grand ultimate—"faith in God, and a haven of rest." All the little streams of life, on which we sail, flow into the great river of God, and the ocean of eternity is the destination of all.

Each man follows his inclinations, though he may think he thwarts them; these are his pursuits of happiness; these are the avenues in which he goes to find the precious boon. Each and every effort, of every one, tends in the direction of natural inclination, the object of which is happiness. We drink when thirsty, eat when hungry, get warm when too cold, and cold when too warm; these are natural demands, and the inclination and effort to obey them is natural too. And so it is in all the actions of life. We may drink too much; if we do, it is but the gratification of an inclination; we may eat too much, and if we do, there is a cause, and there is no cause outside of nature, outside of law, and no nature or law outside of God. We may get too warm, or too cold; if we do, there still, we find, exists in the current of nature the ever-running course of cause and effect; while the life and action of the human heart ever pulsates for happiness.

Every man is launched upon the stream of life; his bark is shaped by his soul's capacities; he meets obstructions, adverse waves, and winds, but, cling however hard he will to the banks of earth, all these tend but to turn him into the deeper current, and he sails more happily and serenely on and on, to the infinite ocean of endless life.

Alice Jones, that farmer's girl, brought up in a log house, puts on her calico dress, and her bonnet with red ribbons, and goes to meeting on Sunday. William Jones, her brother, goes a-fishing. Alice and William both are led in an avenue of happiness as their inclination invites. Law directs both.

Cotton Mather preached eternal damnation of the human family, save a few. Murray preached universal salvation of the human family. Both these men were in the pursuit of happiness, governed each by the law of the peculiar organization and development of their spirits, each obeying their inclinations, each running in some avenue of the soul after happiness.

Webster, the murderer, sought happiness in one avenue; Webster, the statesman, in another; and Webster, the dictionary-maker, in another; each obeyed the bent of inclination — obeyed the law of their nature; each was in pursuit of happiness.

Patrick pursues happiness in the avenue of his pipe, and Mrs. Patrick in storming the children and Patrick too.

Mary, the amiable young woman, walks gently in an avenue of happiness in obeying and loving her parents, and Sukey, the tomboy, in disobeying and hating them. Flotilda is inclined to be happy in wearing high heels, and dressing better than the other girls, whose fathers are not so rich as her father, while the lowly Emma is inclined to be happy in appearances without attractions, without show, in humility, in loving everybody, and keeping God's commandments, as she thinks. Each walks in an avenue of immediate happiness; neither without obedience to law. Lucy, the courtesan, is led in an avenue of happiness where her inclinations *immediately* direct, with the *deeper* longings of her soul, held for a time in check; and her sister Frances, the faithful wife and mother, in another avenue of happiness, where her inclinations lead.

The man of popularity is inclined in the way of

popularity; he seeks happiness in that avenue; while the man covered all over with scandal and scorn, hated and rejected by all, has no less love of happiness, and is no less faithful to his inclinations, is no less an object of the law that governs him — the law of God that may not be put off.

Willie goes to school and learns his lesson; Joe plays truant and goes a-gunning; Daniel goes to college, and Harry goes to horse races and turkey shoots. What makes these boys different? Inclination. And inclination ever seeks happiness; the nature of the soul-germ makes them what they are, which, in its growth, is ever subject to law.

A man of conscience is faithful to his inclinations,

> ——— "his life is passed
> In justifying and condemning sin."

A man without a conscience is no less faithful to his inclinations; he justifies or condemns no sin. It is pleasant to one man to proclaim his infidelity; it is pleasant to the other man to tell him his destiny is eternal misery, because he don't believe as he does. Each of these men obeys the laws of God in nature; the nature of the soul makes the cause, and law the effect.

Henry Ward Beecher follows in the wake of his natural inclinations; he pursues happiness spontaneously. Peter Mahony does the same thing in a different direction. Theodore Parker says the Church is a fiction, and the Church says Theodore Parker is a demon, and both are in the pursuit of happiness in their vituperations.

Spiritualism is a humbug, say its opposers; Spiritualism is beautiful, say its believers. Nothing is said without a cause, and that cause is in the bosom of the speaker—in nature.

One says that a certain belief is debasing and injurious, and writes "eternal punishment" on it in letters of brimstone. Another says that that same belief is elevating and purifying, and cherishes it in the heart with the fondest affection. Inclination leads us to different avenues of happiness in which difference is the immediate cause of this variety of opinion.

One man loves to get drunk; another hates, detests, abhors, condemns drunkenness; there is a cause for this love in one, and this hate in the other; it is natural inclination seeking happiness in the avenue where nature directs.

One man robs a bank, another builds a meeting-house; one prays, another curses; one grinds the poor, another visits them in the name of Christ, and every one, with no exception, seeks happiness, obedient to natural inclination.

The skilful mariner steers best; but all voyagers on the sea of life are liable to be driven upon quicksands and rocks, by the capricious elements, by storms and winds, in darkness and clouds, which *no human hand can keep back.* The law that governs cannot be put off. The action of the soul is its reaching for happiness, which draws it ever upward. It is only the covering of the soul, the material body and its loves, that is torn, wounded, and injured by shipwrecks and adversity, dislodging its material coverings, and preparing it sooner for freedom—for its garments of enduring beauty.

But what are the consequences of human actions,

for good or for evil? In answer, I ask what are the consequences of the forces of nature? what is the effect of the workings of nature's laws? In the natural inclinations of the human soul in the pursuit of happiness, it heeds not, it *knows not* consequences. The inclinations of men and women are spontaneous, ever and forever; a secret spring lies behind, that moves the tongue, the hands, the feet, and the thoughts to action. We think our actions are self-made, are the fruit of individual effort, but analysis of the operations of life will prove the contrary. If a man resist evil, or what is apparently evil to him, he may think it is himself that does it, but for this there is a natural inclination, a fresh, immediate, unseen cause, that is spontaneous; it is the God-power acting, both in the man that resists evil, and in the man that resists not evil.

> "We do not make our thoughts; they grow in us
> Like grains in wood; the growth is of the skies;
> The skies are of nature: nature is of God."

Has nature consequences? Only the just effect of law. Is there responsibility? None above God's laws in nature; nothing in nature is lost, and nothing can be added to it by man.

> "——— no soul
> Though buried in the centre of all sin,
> Is lost to God ———."

No soul is nearer, or further off from God, for God is everywhere. The law of gravitation makes muddy water run down hill; it makes pure water do the same; the law of cohesion is the same in both, the laws of nature cannot be put off; destiny holds every drop of water. A drop of turbid water makes as pure vapor as the glistening dewdrop makes. God's laws are fixed; they permeate every avenue of space and every particle of matter.

The soul of man, like the drop of water, may be turbid with earthy matter; man knows no law whereby a drop of water may be annihilated, or injured; its elements exist forever, and tend ever to a higher condition. Mix water with the most filthy matter of earth, do with it what you will, and the water is unhurt, uninjured; its nature tends upward; is expansive; it rises unseen in greater magnitude, with increased power, and is no less pure because it has been mixed with earth. It is the same with the soul; it exists in matter; its tendency is ever upward to a higher existence; ever increasing in purity and in power as it rises above matter.

The soul is no less a subject of the laws of God than is the raindrop, or the dewdrop. God is infinite in his attributes, and when we can see God's power and wisdom in every manifestation of motion and life, ever tending upward to a better and higher existence, like little children we shall fall into the arms of trust, and in confidence have faith in God. When the soul has grown to that condition of beauty, where it sees God in all nature, the ruling hand of God in all life, then it sails serenely on the great river of God, which is the great source of happiness into which all life is tending, and to which all life is flowing.

5

NATURE.

Nature is both the visible and the invisible world. From infinite to infinite; from unconceived nothingness to unmeasured reality, nature holds dominion. God is nature, and all that he produces is nature; outside of nature exists nothing. The toys and foibles of childhood are nature's possessions. The toys and foibles of manhood are nature's possessions. All the beautiful cathedrals, the elegant churches, the magnificent halls, the costly palaces, the many houses of merchandise, and the multitude of ships floating upon the seas, are the possessions of nature, are realities to physical existence; but all these are toys and playthings of the infant soul of man, and, like the foibles of childhood, will not be of use when the soul is grown to spirit manhood. All the trees that grow on the earth, we say, are the possessions of nature; and we may say that all the things that are made of trees are, in their productions, of nature too; all the treasures that lie in the bosom of the earth, the whole catalogue of minerals, we say, are the possessions of nature. And we may say that all the things that are made from minerals are, in their production, the possessions of nature too; for nature, through human contrivance, extends her handiwork a little further, and we have all the productions of art. All art is the lawful possession of nature.

All things are nature, or of nature. The gewgaws and the tinsels of fashion, are no less the possessions of nature than is honest labor and useful toil; than is the wild flower and the water lily. The broad road that leads to the destruction of material glory, is nature's road. The straight and narrow path that leads to material excellence and earthly happiness, is nature's path. The avenues of nature are infinite in numbers and in varieties. The wayward and the erring, the virtuous and the just, all walk in the avenues of nature as nature directs. The intemperate man is held and guided by nature, and the temperate man is held and guided by nature no less. The courtesan is an object of nature, so is the woman of virtue. Human restraint is natural, and so is human indulgence. The happy man is made happy by nature; the man of suffering is made to suffer by nature.

All the religions of the earth are the possessions of nature. All the creeds and beliefs that exist, and all opposition to creeds and beliefs that exist, are the possessions of nature. The man who thinks that he is excellent and good, and expects a greater reward for himself from the storehouse of heaven, than he expects for others, is an object of nature, just as much as the man is, who thinks that he is no better than other men are, and claims that all are created and guided by the same Father, with equal rights and privileges — with equal claims on heaven and eternal happiness.

All the wars of religious opinions, all the hatred that flows therefrom, and all the bloodshed of nations, are the possessions of nature, just as much as is all the concord of human souls, all the love, the peace, the joy that has ever existed in the bosom of humanity.

Nature holds humanity with a stern and inflexible hand; and outside the grasp of nature is no existence.

What is nature? It is the manifestation of God's power and God's wisdom acting upon all matter and upon all life. Nature bears to us the evidence of unmeasured power and of unmeasured wisdom. All the evidence we have of an infinite God exists in nature.

We ask, is nature right in all her works? And with an emphasis too big for human utterance, the intuition of the soul of man responds, yes; and reason must echo the response, for in nature's bosom is held illimitable power and illimitable wisdom. All nature is right, for all nature is the handiwork of God; and there is no wrong or evil in God; there is no wrong or evil in nature, and there is no place for evil except it be in nature or in God; there is no place outside of nature for wrong or evil to exist, and thus it is a plain conclusion that whatever exists is right.

Deep hidden lies the main-spring of life, the ever-acting laws of God in nature, that move with unerring certainty the vast and complicated machinery of all creation. The foolish and the wise, the young and the old, the good and the bad — each, one and all, are wheels in the mechanism of life, all in gear, all moved by the main-spring of spirit power, the power of nature. If we examine the mechanism of life, we shall see the connections, and the mighty workings of this unseen power. Spiritualism takes us by the hand and leads us to examine and understand the great and beautiful works of nature, where the hand of God is made visible in all things; his wisdom, power, and munificence, so generous and beneficent, that the heart of man will pulsate *faith in God*, while the tongue is silent, and cannot speak the heart's emotion.

NATURE RULES.

The condition of life, which makes us conscious of the existence of apparent evil, is necessary; so is the unhappiness that is the consequence of this consciousness. The perception of evil is the necessity of a condition; it belongs to a degree of the soul's progress; it is the effect of an early process of the soul's growth. It is right, for it is a necessity. But when the soul shall attain a higher degree of progression, the perception of evil will become extinct, and in its place will come the very consoling, happy, heavenly thoughts and words, "*All is right*" —

"All discord's harmony" *then* "understood."

All goodness is spontaneous; all else is fiction; all evil is a fiction. All nature is good; and in nature we have both day and night. Is the day better than the night? Is not each a necessity? Is not each good? We have sunshine and clouds; the clouds are necessary to give the earth rain, and rain is as necessary as the sunshine to make the earth bring forth her supplies, which are necessary for our wants. Both sunshine and clouds are good.

The earth yields poisonous and nutritious plants— thorns and roses; lions and lambs; worms and butterflies; serpents and sweet singing birds. Life is everywhere in varied forms; on the land, in the sea, and in the air; and man, still the work of nature's God, crowns the whole. All these are nature's productions, and if we know not the use of each, let us not say that nature is wrong, but rather our knowledge is limited.

> "The wings of Time are black and white,
> Pied with morning and with night.
> Mountain tall and ocean deep,
> Trembling balance duly keep."

Life is made of *ups* and *downs;* for every excess in nature there is a corresponding want; if tides are high in one place, they are low in another; if there is a mountain, there is a corresponding valley; the extremes of winter cold have corresponding extremes of summer heat. In all nature there is an equipoise, an even balance.

Humanity is a natural production, and in it the same laws hold good that govern matter in lower conditions in nature. For every splendid mansion there is a humble cottage; for excess and superabundance of the necessary things of life, there is want and deprivation; for excessive wealth there is excessive poverty; for excessive goodness, there is corresponding want of goodness; there is genius and stupidity; intelligence and ignorance; there is an excess of pleasure, but never without a corresponding excess of pain somewhere. The hand of justice holds the scales of human happiness and suffering, and they are balanced in evenness.

The same law holds good when we come to an individual man. *A man* is a microcosm, a little universe; he is a world in himself. God is as infinite in littleness, as in greatness; as perfect in little man, as he is in worlds of magnitude that swing, balanced in perfect order, in limitless space. The law of justice, the law of evenness, balances the work, the mechanism of the human body and the human soul. For every excellence in any man, there is a corresponding defect; for every good there is a corresponding evil, so called, perhaps not known; for every excess of virtue there is a vice, so called, it may be, latent; for every tear shed, there is a gem of beauty; for every pain, there is a fragrant flower of undying freshness, a truth gained; for every sorrow, there is a joy; for every loss, there is a gain. In man exist no excesses without a corresponding balance. Nature is a leveller, and balances every thing; allows no exceptions; no monopolies; no more in an individual man than she does in the whole range of her vast dominions beneath man. Shall man contend with nature? No; he cannot, for it is the power of God in nature that makes him what he is. Let nature stop her work in the vegetable kingdom one year, and all life on earth ceases. Let nature stop her work in animal life one hour, and all men are numbered with the dead. Let nature cease to do her work for one moment in the physical world, and the universe is chaos.

Do not nature's laws, then, command our attention and our reverence? Man is ruled by nature, and nature to man is destiny; and a distinct view of destiny is a revelation to man, of *faith in God.*

Can a man influence or alter a law of nature? Can a man, if he tries as hard as he can, make the earth revolve the other way, so that the sun will rise in the west and set in the east? or, can he stop the ebbing and flowing of the tide? Can he add to or take from a single ray of the great sun that shines upon us? Can he make the attraction of gravitation stop, or an atom of matter cease to exist? *I don't believe he can.* Neither do I believe that there is one single law in nature anywhere, that he can influence or alter in any way, or in any degree, made manifest in man. Man is as immediately and as perfectly under the influence of these laws as is the sun, the earth, and the tides. The nature of man's soul is progressive; he is ever changing; he has intelligence and consciousness. There is a condition, a degree in his progression, where he *believes* that he has power above and independent of the power of nature; for the more perfect development of his identity, or his self-hood, or, for some cause still hidden, we shall see this belief a necessity of a degree of progress — a manifestation of that degree which is natural. No one moment of time does the soul cease to move; and onward and upward with all things is its course forever. And as man's consciousness becomes more clear in viewing the laws of nature, he will sooner or later see that her work is right, balanced justly, in equity; he will see a hand of Divine Intelligence made visible as he traces the working of this power in the steps of his soul's progress, all ultimating in his highest good. Then, and not before, as he reviews the past, will he see that God has purposes, and nature works them out, and the means to work out his ends are what we call *good* and *evil*, or rather good and evil are the effect of this work; each one and both are necessary to the end. What we call evil is as much the effect of a means in working out the purposes of creation, the ultimate purity of man, as good is. When we begin to comprehend the *perfect* power of God in nature, we shall not say that aught that is of God is wrong, for we have faith in his perfect power, and say that it is right.

WHAT APPEARS TO BE EVIL IS NOT EVIL.

In taking the ground that there is no evil, spirit in all cases is the standard. All things in the material world are the product of spirit. Spirit is real and eternal, and is always good. The soul of man is man's reality. The soul is all there is of man that is valuable and enduring. The soul is unseen, undefined, and cannot be judged of by our earthly reason. Spiritual perception — intuition alone can recognize its real existence.

All that our earthly eyes see of human existence are effects of the soul made manifest through material things, and like material things these effects possess the properties of change and decay; inharmony, conflict, and darkness. The shadows of matter shut out from our spiritual vision the reality of spirit existence, and these shadows we call evil. As the soul grows out of earthly love, the shadows break away, and all becomes beautiful and true.

In this earlier condition of our earthly existence, shadows have seemed real, and have been taken for actual causes, when they were really *only* effects. Spirit has seemed to be an effect, when it was really only the cause. The conditions of life that we call evil, we must pass in our progress, — we cannot avoid them, — and in doing this we must suffer pain. I cannot think that, in the earlier condition of progress, there is *any* advance without pain; every pulsation of progression is followed by suffering; we never seek this pain, so the pulsations of progress are always as involuntary to us, as are the pulsations of our hearts. There is an unseen Power that makes our hearts beat, and there is just as much, some unseen power that makes our souls progress. We only know of this power by its effects.

What appears to us evil, is absolutely an effect of soul-growth, or is so inseparably connected with soul-growth that the two cannot be separated. I would not say now, as I have in former articles, that suffering is the cause of soul-growth; but I will go one step further into hidden realities, and say that suffering is an *effect*, and is a positive *evidence* of soul-development. The soul begins its growth clothed in a garment of material love, and as it grows it breaks the threads of this garment, one by one, and every break of every thread produces a pain that we must bear. It is only the breaking of the threads, all the threads in the garment of our earthly love, that makes up the whole sum of earthly suffering, and what we call evil is the proximate cause of suffering. It is the breaking up of all earthly love that gives the soul a new birth — a birth into the world of light and freedom; a world to which it ever tends, and in which it first finds a real consciousness of its true existence. In our earthly existence, the soul is only growing in the dark womb of physical nature, and when earthly love is broken it has its birth into real life. The whole process of the *utero* gestation of the soul in its earthly existence is darkness and conflict, out of which its own inherent powers, forced by the unseen laws of nature, struggle to gain its lawful freedom. All this darkness and this conflict we have called evil, because pain is thereby felt. But in darkness we have been unable to see that all these things are natural and necessary — absolutely essential to the condition of the soul, while it exists in the darkness of the physical world. So the appearance of evil, when seen in the light of the new-born spirit, in the light of spirit reality, is recognized only as a necessary shadow of matter. Thus it is a reasonable conclusion, that what appears to us evil, is not evil, but is positively a necessity for greater good in the wise ordering of the power that makes the soul's development.

SPIRITUAL COMMUNICATION.

The following communication from a spirit was given through the mediumship of Mrs. J. S. Adams, in March, 1855:—

Bright fancy wooed my soul one day, and my spirit flew with wings ideal, and roved among the bright, the beautiful, the loving things that God has made. I gathered me roses only, and left the thorns; I only drank from laughing brooks; I ranged amid the universe of love; I went to gather flowers and garlands, for fancy would not let me look on shadows; and I thought within me, if there is so much beauty in the universe to be found, why will the eye scan o'er the hideous things? If roses bloom with thorns beside them, why not take the roses and leave the thorns? This was the language of the beautiful.

Then reason bounded o'er the wilderness, the desert, the wild-wood, and, gazing around, saw nature grow in what seemed all confusion, flowers delicately blooming in unsightly soil. Still onward reason flew, while fancy tarried with flowers. Must reason traverse o'er these wilds alone? Will fancy not come forth and chant some melting cadence, and crown the brow of reason with roses?

My soul with reason flew, and with philosophy I traversed the desert and the wilderness, and found strange beauties that fancy's eye had not discovered. I saw within the thorn what made the rose so sweet.

I saw why shadows came embracing moonbeams. I saw why bright and mossy vines clung over old, decaying wood. Where fancy failed to go, wisdom led me forth, and in my spirit chimed, "*All, all is beautiful.*"

Then sympathy and love came forth, and I saw tears and sorrow and sighing; then fancy whispered within my soul, " This is not bright and beautiful." Then wisdom came, and fancy fled. A brilliant star upon her brow threw light upon the scene, and I saw why sorrow and sadness were around me. It was a key-note in God's great harmony of creation to lead my spirit forth in love, affection, and sympathy. For what were these faculties lodging within me? Were they not to go forth when sorrow was sighing? And with wisdom I saw that this was also beautiful.

I saw a dark and hideous form borne to the spirit-world. He came in loneliness and in sorrow. I looked again; there came a bright and beauteous form to join a seraph host above. There were pearl-drops glittering round her brow, made of the tears of affection. I gazed upon them long, and all that was beautiful and bright and lovely within my soul, drew no thought to the heaven-born host, where the new-born spirit had joined; while sympathy, tenderness, and compassion drew my spirit-thoughts to the sad, dejected form that was borne to the spirit-world. Fancy said, let us join the shining host; but wisdom prompting, spoke within my soul, and bade me seek the weary, the downcast, the sad one. And I saw from the light of the golden stars that all in this was beautiful and bright; that the shining host above drew out my finer throes. My spirit melted with deep love, and joined the sad one's woes, and there was beauty, heavenly beauty, in the thought that I could aid that saddened form, and some day see him join that beauteous choir, that throng of light to which that spirit from the same earth has gone. The one departed from out the garden of flowers, the other came forth from briers and thorns. And the rose and the thorn were all made beautiful. I had learned a lesson of life. And I said within my soul, O God, there is naught but harmony, and a bright and circular gradation of beauty that winds to thy central glory.

CAUSE OF WHAT WE CALL EVIL.

> "Men speculate on right and wrong
> As upon day and night, forgetting both
> Have but one cause, and that the same — God's will."

WHAT is evil? Evil may be defined as being those manifestations of life that are repulsive to the heavenly desires of the human heart. What is the cause of so-called evil? In one word this question may be answered, viz., *nature.* Without reserve, boldly and fearlessly, I solemnly give in my testimony, and swear, that evil is a natural production. The operations of nature gave birth to it, and it rises up from the workings of her mighty machinery, and, like vapor, dissipates. Nature produces every thing that we call evil, no less than that we call good.

> "God shows his face to us no less in darkness
> Than in the light."

It would be childish to say that behind the blow that murdered a man there was not a cause, the effect of which was the blow, and the consequence the murder. Nature has hidden springs. There lies a brain of peculiar organization behind the hand that gave the blow, which produced the murder. That brain was made by nature. Unseen currents of vitality run through that brain, and nature gives these currents, and makes them flow. We cannot see them; they stimulate the brain, and the brain acts as servant to these currents, according to its organization, formation, and capacity. These currents of life come into the brain, and run down through the feet and hands of the murderer; and they are servants too. They use the feet to carry the murderer to the scene of murder, and the hands to do the deed. And the man we call a free moral agent, kills another man that we call a free moral agent. This deed we call evil. What is the cause? Nature. What is nature? God. And is nature wrong? Is God, the great main-spring of nature, wicked? Is there that in nature which needs remedial agents, to be administered by the feeble hand of man? The desires of men, and the inclinations of men — from whence come they? From God, direct and immediate. Every desire of the human heart runs as natural and as true to the laws of God in nature, as the stream of water runs obedient to the laws of God in gravitation — sometimes turbid, in darkness, and in miry places, and sometimes in sunshine and in crystal purity, over clean sand and pebbles. The little rivulet has its origin in nature — it is moved by nature — its windings, and its gurglings, its foamings and its splashings, are all the effects of natural laws. Dam it up, and by the laws of nature it rises above the obstruction and flows on; it mingles with other waters, and still obedient to the laws of nature, it flows on and on, and is lost in the ocean of its destination.

The human soul is like a stream of time. It governs itself no more than does the little rivulet of the earth; but like it, it is held perfectly obedient to *unseen laws.* The hand of destiny holds the rivulet, and the hand of destiny holds the souls of men. The stream goes zigzag; man is wayward, and goes zigzag. It bears bubbles on its surface and they break; human life has bubbles, and they break. The stream dashes furiously over the precipice, and moves faster on its course in consequence of its foaming, dashing fury; the peaceful course of human life is thus broken, by what we call these damning evils; the waters of life are thereby agitated, not injured; stagnation is arrested, and progression is accelerated thereby; it moves more rapidly on to its destination in consequence of the moral falls which break its peaceful flow. Then the stream flows calm and tranquil, peacefully and beautifully; so the course of human life is sometimes calm, tranquil, peaceful, and beautiful. This is "good," we say; this is "holiness and righteousness," we say. But in this peaceful flow the soul moves more slowly on to its destination of eternal beauty; its earthly windings are lengthened, and its heaven is later reached.

"Evil" is the rapid fall in the stream of time; good is its peaceful flow. Evil shortens our earthly love; good lengthens it. The stream of life flows on unbidden and ungoverned by man, but it flows in obedience to the laws of God in nature.

What is the cause of what we call evil? Was an evil deed ever committed without a cause of sufficient power to produce the deed? No philosopher can answer, yes. Then where lies the cause, and where had it its origin? We say, in yielding to temptation; in some deed of evil that has preceded. Go back another step — where had that temptation, and the yielding to it, an origin? and keep going back, step by step, and at last we must conclude that every cause lies far back in the bosom of God.

The cause of "evil" lies beyond the reach of human vision as developed in the sensuous world; far beyond the boundaries of human philosophies. In the bosom of intuition we shall find it.

EVIL DOES NOT EXIST.

"There's not a place on earth's vast round,
In ocean deep, or air,
Where skill and wisdom are not found,
For God is everywhere.

"Around, beneath, below, above—
Wherever space extends,
There Heaven displays its boundless love,
And power with goodness blends."

That which seems to us evil, is not evil intrinsically; it is only the natural operation of things for the production of good. Evil is the effect of a means, whose end is as great in goodness as is the magnitude of the apparent evil.

The reason why we call certain actions evil, is because we know no better; is because we have not a capacity to see, comprehend, and understand the wisdom of God in the mighty workings of his power. No one can deny that there is an unseen power and an unseen wisdom at work in the manifestations of life, that we see everywhere around us. This wisdom and this power transcends human wisdom and human power, as the magnitude of uncounted worlds transcends the magnitude of a single man. Has finite man confidence in this power and this wisdom? We say that God is infinite in these attributes. Have we faith in his infinite power and wisdom? Have we faith in God? If we have, we feel safe, perfectly safe;

we are happy; we have found a heaven of rest. We see what is apparently wrong, and conclude that it is for wise ends; for it is all the work of this Infinite Wisdom and Infinite Power. We are little; God is great. We cannot see his mighty purposes, his schemes and plans; we cannot understand by viewing a single link, or many links, in the interminable chain of cause and effect, for what purpose the whole long chain is to be used. If we have perfect confidence in God, we love him through all his works; no less in what seems to us evil, than in what seems to us good.

The firemen blow up a house to prevent the spread of a terrible conflagration in a densely populated city; the deed is executed in the higher wisdom of larger human intelligence. Smaller intelligence that could not see the wisdom of the deed and knew not for what end it was done, might think this blowing up of a house, voluntarily and purposely, an evil, while the end was really for good.

A wise physician draws out the deadly inflammation from the vital organs of his patient upon the skin by a blister, and he sees in this lesser evil a means of greater good; while the unintelligent, the uninformed sees this terrible inflammation, this awful blister that the doctor has made, and without hesitation pronounces it an evil. The blister works out good in the end.

The boy, under the lash of his father's correction, never thinks that whipping is the best thing his father can do for him; the whipping, he thinks, is a cruel evil; he knows less than his father does; he sees that an evil which his father sees a good.

A failure in a successful business often brings out

the true man; it is the best thing that can happen. But you cannot make a man believe this, till he grows large in spirit, and can see it; he thinks that it is the Devil that causes the failure, and the failure is an evil; when perhaps it has been planned and executed by his redeeming angels, to lead him more rapidly on his journey of progression.

Thus it is in some of the little things of life that to ignorance appear evil, in the light of intelligence appear wise and good.

I feel an abiding confidence that, when we shall grow pure in heart, we shall see God in the light of truth, in good no less than in evil; and we shall see all the works of God as having been planned and executed in wisdom, for the highest good of all men.

UNHAPPINESS IS NECESSARY.

UNHAPPINESS is the product of soul development, and is always in its time and place; it is a lawful effect of the soul's growth, and in no possible contingency, by material efforts, can it be lessened or avoided. Unhappiness is just as right as happiness is. And if unhappiness is right, the cause that produced it must also be right, which cause we have called *evil.* We always seek happiness and try to avoid unhappiness; but our efforts to influence the growth of the soul that produces these effects, are futile ever. Our efforts affect our material existence—not the soul's existence. Our happiness and our unhappiness are always the effect of the sure laws of God, in nature, acting upon our souls. It is a hand of love that holds the cup of bitterness to our lips, no less than it is a hand of love that fills our cup of joy to overflowing. And blessed be that hand which gives us both pain and joy. Both are right.

When we suffer pain, it is hard for us to see a hand of goodness in its ministration; but by careful reflection we sometime shall see that pain has always been for good; and when we see this, then, if we *could,* we would not take it back. How many afflictions of our past lives can we recount already, and see that in each has been a means that has benefited the soul. And we have powers, but feebly developed yet, to read the anatomy of cause and effect in the chain of human life, and less have we powers developed to read and understand the physiology of soul progress, the functions of every cause and effect, and the mysterious sympathy that runs through the whole.

Disease is the result of a means of the soul's growth. It is as natural to a certain condition of life as health is, and to that condition in which it exists it is necessary and inevitable; it is lawful and right. The painful influences of poison are natural, necessary, and inevitable to that condition, where we say that ignorance makes its influences a blind accident. There is no accident in nature, and all that is, is nature.

Murder has no influence upon the soul; it is a thing of the material world in its influences. It has no influence upon spiritual existence of which it is an effect. When the murderer kills his brother, he strikes a blow that will paralyze every love of his own earthly existence. Then the affections of his soul must cling to something; and if his love of earth becomes broken by the awful deed of murder, and the consequent punishment that he meets, spiritual things are next grasped, and perhaps sooner grasped for the commission of the deed. The murderer does his deeds in darkness; he does not commit the deed with a view to advance the progress of his soul. He is moved by an unseen and irresistible power to commit what seems to us the "*evil*" deed. Every murder that ever was committed has been inevitable; in the bosom of nature has existed the lawful cause, of which murder has been the effect. The causes of nature and the effects of nature are always right.

Now, reader, do not go away and say that this book

recommends murder. It only talks about murder as it is, and of all other "evils" as they are.

Theft and robbery are effects of a cause; the effects are in the material world, the causes in the spiritual world. Stealing is the work of nature too, in humanity, and it will exist as long as the condition exists in nature, of which it is a necessity. Stealing is right to its condition, and, in that condition, by the inflexible power of nature's laws, it must exist; therefore, it is right. All efforts made against the crime of stealing are also right.

Intemperance, debauchery, and degradation never have had existence without a cause to produce them. Nature is their father and mother.

Thorns and thistles, poisonous plants, and poisonous animals, are no less the productions of nature than are fragrant flowers, nutritious vegetables, and useful animals.

So are the actions of men and women that we call evil the product of nature, as much as are the actions that we call good. Is nature wrong? No; for all the manifestations of nature are the manifestations of God. God is good — not evil. I would not try to push away the hand of love that holds me. Then,

> "Press close bare-bosomed night!
> Press close magnet nourishing night.

All crime is rewarded with suffering; "the wages of sin is death," pain, and misery; and sin, pain, and misery are means to free the soul. Thus it is that crime becomes a fruitful means of good, and we see —

> "Discord is harmony not understood."

In a higher condition of human life there is no crime, and to this condition humanity rises only by pain and suffering.

The hungry man suffers; but the sufferings of hunger are waves of progress that shall enable the soul sooner to feed on those drops of eternal wisdom, which shall nourish it forever.

The toiling slave suffers; but the sufferings of a toilsome life are breaking the fetters of earthly love, whereby the soul shall be sooner set free to wander "at its own sweet pleasure," in the

"Gardens where angels walk, and seraphs are the wardens."

The widows and the orphans suffer; but God and angels love them, and administer suffering to them to earlier prepare them for the full company of congenial souls, where there shall be no more death, no sighs, no sorrows, no unsatisfied desires. It is progression through suffering that shall make widows and orphans angels; and so it is of all earth's children.

That young woman suffers who makes the rich man's shirts; who, by constant toil all day and half the night, is scarcely able to feed her sickly mother and herself, and wear the cheapest fabric for her clothes. The midnight lamp reflects the hectic flush, her aching, tired shoulders — these in silence proclaim her suffering. Every pain she bears cuts asunder a thread of love that binds her soul to earth, and it shall mount on wings of spirit-love, to soar away in freedom, sooner for her suffering.

And thus it is with all the sufferings of human souls. Suffering is incident to every place and every condition of the earth.

Humanity progresses ever, but never without pain and conflict. Shall I curse the means that work out my greatest good? Shall I denounce and resist evil when it brings suffering, which suffering must be identified with my progression?

Evil is held in check, or is dealt out to humanity by a hand of wisdom and power. Evil comes not by human will, or by human effort. No man suffers by his own desires; no man is happy at his own pleasure. No human effort can stay or advance the tide of evil that flows over humanity; it is God-given and God-directed. God is good, and doeth all things well. I thank God for human progress; I thank God for the proximate cause of human progress, which is suffering; and I thank God for the cause of suffering, which is sin.

The elements of drunkenness, of prostitution, of murder, and of crime exist in the world on the existing plane of human progress; and while these elements hold a place in humanity, their manifestations in the great work of human life are inevitable.

It is folly to say that these evils are enhanced or diminished by all that may be said or written on the subjects pertaining to them. A careful review of the history of the past shows that the world has been flooded with preaching and talking against all kinds of evil, while they still, unmitigated, keep on untouched, uninfluenced.

Let no one think that this article advocates drunkenness, prostitution, crime, or oppression. It has nothing to do with increasing or diminishing these so-called evils, nor is it possible for it to have any effect in either direction. The elements of evil are integral parts in the material and early existence of the human soul; and evil made manifest is the natural operation of the soul's progression. The progression of man is the great purpose of life, and all the manifestations of life are the effect of means working to this end. So every thing that we call wrong and evil is absolutely good.

HARMONY AND INHARMONY.

So long as the phantom *Evil* is seen, its condemnation is inevitable; and so long as the shadows of earthly love linger in the soul, so long this phantom called Evil is visible. Opposition is an enemy to peace, and condemnation is the fruit of opposition. In a condition of perfect peace there is no opposition to any thing that exists. The soul that is in harmony with every thing, sees every thing as being right, and nothing as being wrong, or evil. It is the soul of inharmony that sees almost every thing as being wrong; and it is the condition of the soul that sees inharmony, that is inharmonious; the things seen outside the soul that sees them are only *seen* to be evil, they are not really so. So the condemnation of an evil is only a chastisement for the soul's self that condemns.

The soul grows up through the inharmony and the darkness of materialism, and, while it is thus growing, it sees and condemns evil. As the soul grows to recognize the reality of spirit, as it ever will more and more, the shadow called Evil lessens, and finally, in the undimned light of the spirit, it sees no evil.

Medium developments are spiritual unfoldings in the soul; an increasing recognition of spiritual realities; a constantly increasing harmony of the soul with all conditions and all things in existence. The best and the truest medium for the reception and transmission of spiritual truths, is the medium who is in perfect harmony with all things — who sees no evil, no wrong, and has no opposition, no condemnation for any thing that exists. Such a medium, in a perfectly normal condition, can talk with angels face to face — can read human hearts without the aid of words — can command any truth from the spiritual universe that it has a desire to command; that it has a capacity to receive.

Peter J. Ballard, of Marblehead, when entranced, or under the control of spirits, made medium developments to consist of seven classes, corresponding with the seven notes which make the octave in music, and from which the different sounds that make all the melody in music proceed. Every person on earth is a medium, and is in some one of these seven classes of medium development. The average development of the human family, is between the first and second, is in the second. Each class of medium developments is characterized by certain manifestations peculiar to itself. And every class is characterized by an absence of *perfect* harmony, until the seventh is fully developed. When the soul has passed this last development, it has made the octave in which harmony exists, and the soul is thereby tuned to melody; it is then in harmony with all life and all its manifestations. There can be no discord, no inharmony, no evil to the perfect development of these seven classes of mediumship.

This classification of medium development serves at least to convey some idea of the growth of the soul into a harmonious and melodious development. To play the tune of life harmoniously, and sing the theme of life melodiously, we must first have exercise on all the notes in the octave, and thereby gain the mastery of the various sounds. In this exercise there must be discord and inharmony, but when each note upon the music-staff of life is mastered, the melody of life begins, and in harmony we chant

"Whatever is, is right."

"All is beautiful that beauty sees."

THE SOUL'S PROGRESS.

The soul's progress is and has been the great subject of all recognized religions throughout the world.

The aim of all religions is to make the actions of life good and excellent while the soul inhabits its tenement of clay; believing that by so doing the soul is made better; is better prepared for its existence after death. The ground, I believe, has always been taken, that the soul has been influenced for good or for evil by contact with men and things; that by bad influences it is degraded and retarded in its progress, and by good influences it is advanced and elevated. Such is the doctrine of all *desires* that bear the name of "*religion*." All doctrines I fully accept as being necessary effects of the soul's progress, no doctrine or belief being wrong to the cause that produced it. But all doctrines being manifested through matter, are, like all matter, changeable and perishing.

We have honestly and necessarily thought that the soul has been influenced by doctrines, and can be. But we have claimed, at the same time, that the soul is of eternity, which time cannot obliterate or destroy. If it is, how can it be influenced by that which changes and perishes? I cannot see, if the soul is immortal, how things that are not immortal can have any influence upon it — how its effects, which are perishing, can in any possible way influence its progress, which is eternal. If the soul is unseen and eternal, then that which is unseen and eternal alone must influence it, and be the cause of its progress. If the soul can be influenced by doctrines and beliefs; by "wrong and evil;" by human actions; by the manifestations of human life in matter, all of which are ephemeral, "passing away, passing away"—then, like that which influences it, it must be ephemeral, not immortal.

By no human action is the soul made better or worse; by no human voice or hand is the soul advanced or retarded in its eternal progress; no deed of human life can stay its upward march or help it on. Too mighty, too eternal is the soul, to be influenced by things of time; by doctrines, beliefs, preaching, or writing; by the friction of matter, its rise or fall, its riches or poverties, its glory or its degradation. The human soul! the immortal, beautiful soul! Triumphant over death and hell, it must rise; and surely, over all the fleeting things of earth also, it *must* rise, triumphant — seed of eternal life, planted by the finger of God in his own garden, to bloom in unfading freshness forever!

What is the cause and effect of the progress of the human soul? No human tongue can answer this question, for the answer would cover a knowledge of the limitless area of infinity. There is no beginning, there is no end, to the philosophy of the soul's growth; no man knows the port from whence it started, nor the haven to which it is destined.

The soul had its creation in unconsciousness; it wakes up in its progress; it but dimly discerns the fact of its existence at first; the shadows of matter and the clouds of earth protect for a while its young and tender perception from the dazzling realities of its unmeasured glories. Time strengthens its vision; clouds and shadows disappear as it strengthens; and a conscious perception of its own immortality opens upon its deep and ardent longings in the light of spiritual realities.

Our perceptions of the reality of the soul, and its eternal relations, are exceedingly limited, because our vision is yet unopened; we are yet almost shrouded in the darkness of matter, with its changing, perishing philosophies. Gleams of spirit-light, soul-light, now and then, in pencil rays, shine from within us. We comprehend but faintly the glorious reality. As we pass from feeble spirit-infancy, to stronger spirit-childhood, and then to stronger spirit-manhood, we grow to bear the increasing beauty and effulgence of spiritual light. Some time, we shall intuitively know a new philosophy, that, on the wings of desire, shall leap to catch and hold forever the truths of God. This shall be the philosophy of the soul.

I have a powerful and abiding conviction that our wildest and most extravagant conceptions of the yet unspoken beauties of the human soul are infinitely small when compared with the magnitude of its reality. And to philosophize upon that which we know but ittle of, which we have not seen, and which our conceptions have even failed to reach, is impossible to do with any degree of perfectness. But with what little light of immortality our souls, by natural growth, have caught, we have a right, in the baby-house of our spiritual existence, to philosophize as babies do, with a baby-house philosophy, which philosophy is of the material world.

There, surely, is some power that has created the

soul; and as *surely there must be* some power that guides the soul. This power is before and above the soul's volition, beyond the soul's control.

We did not command the creation of our souls, nor do we control the power that created them; and no more can we command or control the same power — the power which makes them grow. The soul and all its forces are beyond and above all the influences of time, and the powers of the material world.

We have confidence that, in the ordering of Infinite Wisdom, the soul is necessarily planted in matter to begin its growth in darkness and in conflict — there to grow, and to bud, and then to blossom in the sunshine of heaven. How this is, the *whys* and the *wherefores*, the cause and the effect, lies far beyond the present development of our senses.

Our thoughts run out on spirit-life as gleams of spirit-truth shine in; and gleams of spirit-truth shine in our souls (or out), as the soul by its natural growth, breaks the earthly covering in which it germinates.

The beauty of the material world is one beauty; the beauty of the spiritual world is another beauty. The growth of the spirit breaks the beauty of the material. The nut-shell is beautiful, but it holds a germ of life within that is more beautiful. Hidden forces make that germ expand; this expansion breaks the shell and spoils it; and from this germ new life springs forth; the germ grows to buds and flowers, and their emanations of fragrance and beauty go *up* to live forever. In this process is struggle, antagonism, opposition and conflict in darkness; all this is done by a power that is a miracle to humanity; we know nothing of the first cause and of the final effect.

By the same unseen power and wisdom the soul is produced and covered in the material shell of earthly love to protect the germ for a time. But when it grows, it breaks the shell of material love; makes it look bad; spoils it. Human actions that we call *wrong*, *evil*, *devilish*, only produce the cracks and breaks of this shell. The soul that germinates earliest and with the greatest vigor, is in the man who looks the worst, and acts the worst, to the eyes of the material world. The man who is most perfect and beautiful in the material world, loves earth the most. The man who is most broken and deformed in the material world, loves earth the least. In the latter the germination and growth of the soul within has burst the covering of his earthly love; this man, we say, "is religiously and morally bad; is on a very low plane;" while, in the former, the germination and growth of the soul within is a little later, and has not yet broken a fibre of the coverings of material beauty. This man, we say, "is religiously and morally good; his soul is progressed up very high." The growth of the soul affects the things of this world; but the things of this world cannot, in any possible way, affect the growth of the soul. All that makes the soul grow is an unseen power that yet lies behind the curtain of our vision, over which our *will* and our *hands* can have no influence.

We wait for that day to dawn upon us when the curtain of darkness will rise, and we shall see all things in intuitive soul-light, existing in truth and beauty. Then we shall review the past, and see that

"All nature flows in rapturous lay,
Life beams in one eternal ray."

INTUITION.

Intuition alone is the basis on which is reared the superstructure of a positive knowledge of immortality. Intuition is the literature and the science of the soul; it is the philosophy and the logic of the spirit; it is the Bible of God, in which the soul of man alone can read the truths of eternal life. Intuition is conscious existence; it is thought, feeling, and desire. All human intelligence is the production of intuition; all the knowledge of the material world is the offal of intuition.

I desire immortality, and in that desire I have the intuitive evidence of immortality. I desire to commune with angels, and in that desire I have the intuitive evidence of the existence of angels; in that desire I do absolutely commune with them. We long and desire to grasp the unseen beauties of spirit-life, and in this longing is the absolute beginning of the possession of what the soul longs for; in this longing exists the intuitive preception of the reality.

"I want to talk with my mother," said a young man to me, twenty times in the course of an hour's conversation. (His mother was dead, and he loved her.) This young man did not, in an external sense, recognize the fact that the spontaneous desire of his soul to talk with his mother, was absolute *communion* with his mother, by the positive power of intuition.

"Oh, if I could get a communication from my angel

sister!" said Mary B——. Let Mary's fleeting perception of material things grow dim, and with the perception of her soul she will see that in her ardent soul-desires she holds positive communion with her angel sister; with the yet unrecognized power of intuition, she talks with her angel sister, in soul.

Everybody is intuitive. Each spontaneous thought of the soul is of intuition. Each spontaneous feeling of the soul is of intuition. I cannot but believe that the sight of angels and spirits is only the *intensified feeling of their presence*, and this feeling is intuition.

Every real Spiritualist is a Spiritualist alone from intuition, not from external evidence. Philosophy never made a Spiritualist, and never will.

The men and women who deal largely with science and philosophies are the last to recognize intuition; they call it fiction, and Spiritualism they call the same. They deal only with the product of reality, with the trash of matter, and its no less trashy philosophies, that are tangible to physical eyes and physical touch, waiting a while for the recognition of the unseen spirit, and its beautiful intuitions, that produce what they recognize.

Language cannot define the word intuition. The most that can be said, in an attempt to define it, can convey but a faint idea of its reality. We may say that intuition is a conscious perception of truth that is perfectly spontaneous. Intuition is a persuasion of truth developed from the soul, and forever has an abiding place there. Intuition never comes from without into the soul, but is developed from the germ of the soul and comes out.

It is intuition alone that can take cognizance of the positive indestructibility of the soul; that can grasp the fact of the soul's immortality.

It is intuition that recognizes the triumphant power which the soul possesses over all the influences of the material world.

It is intuition that sees the cause of all material existence, in spirit; that sees spirit alone as the real thing of all life.

It is intuition that brings to the soul's consciousness the unutterable beauties that lie in the pathway of its future, eternal progression.

It is intuition that gives the soul a passport to the illimitable fountain of all truth; that opens the gates of heaven, and shuts the gates of hell.

It is intuition that produces philosophies, and buries philosophies with the affections of earthly things; that makes death a pleasant incident, and all life redolent with beauty.

It is intuition that makes us good and true, trustworthy and useful; that develops the stature of true manhood, and makes us what we all are to be — good men and good women in practical deeds, without the trash of external pretence. Philosophies build up pretences, and intuition tears them down.

It may be asked, by what authority thoughts have been uttered that *seem* so opposite to the teachings of the past. This authority is not gleaned from books or any preaching, nor any human philosophies or teaching; but it is the deep and honest convictions of soul. You ask from whence these convictions come? The answer is, they come on the wings of intuition. By intuition we may read the real character of human operations — of men and women; and see the beautiful cause of all the manifestations of life in the physical world, and in that cause see the finger of Infinite Goodness in every thing. It is in this way that we shall fail to discover evil as a thing of existence.

It is intuition alone that shall make clear to us the saying, that "Whatever is, is right." Intuition deals with spirit; philosophy deals with matter. Intuition exists with causes; philosophy with effects. Intuition is the sunlight of truth, that shall endure throughout the daytime of eternal existence; philosophy is the shadow of matter, that shall pass away and be lost in the light of spiritual realities.

RELIGION — WHAT IS IT?

It is the use of a word that gives to us its meaning. From the common walks of every-day practical life I have gathered the meaning of the word *religion;* not from the dictionary, the commentary, or from the pulpit.

Feel the pulse of the throbbing hearts of humanity, and decide whether the following definition of religion is not practically true.

Religion is a *longing* for something not possessed, always accompanied with an effort to satisfy that longing. Religion consists in unsatisfied desires, by which desires we are influenced to actions which may answer the ends of these desires.

What is the religion of human life? It is simply the desires of human life. What are the desires of human life? The desires of human life, without one single exception, are for *happiness.* All men love happiness, and all men seek it. Every human being has desires; each one has desires peculiar to him or herself; and every desire, for the person that desires, is for good, for greater good. A human step is never taken that is not signally to this end in its intention; and we may not say that it will not be in its results.

Every human soul longs for something not yet possessed; and this longing is always joined with the effort to satisfy this longing. No one longs for pain, for misery and suffering, but always for good, for pleasure, for happiness. This is religion; and it is possessed by one no less than by another.

Every human being is moved by natural religion, is governed by natural religion, is obedient to natural inclinations — the source of which is *good*, the desire of which is for *good*, and the end of which, we have confidence, *must be good.*

Our desires lead us through many dark avenues, and the gods of our hearts are sometimes daily changed. Our desires are the gods we worship. Old gods are vanquished as new ones come up. All the avenues of earth lead us to good in the end. There are no vain pathways in the journey of life; all the pathways through which our desires lead us are useful to us, are necessary for us; through them we pass, redeemed, to bliss. Darkness makes the habiliments of mourning; but, as sure as the night is, so sure is the day to follow. Our religion is God-given, and is for a God-purpose always; and we make the sun rise and set no more than we make our religion, our suffering, and our happiness.

There is not a soul on earth that loves not power, and that does not desire it. This desire is religion. Power kills pain and commands happiness.

> " Who would not lift the world with a lever of light?"

Helen says —

> " Oh, I could stand and rend myself with rage
> To think I am so weak, * * *
> While I would be a hand, to sweep from end
> To end, from infinite to infinite."

This wild desire is Helen's religion; and every desire that is not this, is religion; for every one

"Desires that which is most natural."

"Earth hath her deserts mixed with fruitful plains."

And on we go, on to future joys and sorrows, while the past is laid in ruins. The enjoyment of, and thanksgiving for every thing that has passed, is the fruition of religion; and this has come, or *will* come. Every desire is a grand prediction of good to come. Religion is the surest evidence of future happiness, for its demands are always means never too short to reach its ends.

"Words are but motes of thoughts."

Professions are dead cinders of soul-desires of true religion. Religion is not gained by toil; it comes from God — immediate, direct. Desires are not made by us; they grow in us like leaves on trees. Desires are spontaneous; religion is always spontaneous. Religion runs through human hearts like streams of water through woods and fruitful plains, and by their running make their own channels. The running water finds its level by a law of unseen power, defying silently all the dams and forcing-pumps of earth. So religion runs, moved by a silent power, in defiance of all the forcing-pumps and dams of religious appliances, contrivances, rites, forms, and ceremonies.

Religion is like that which feeds it. God feeds it. God is good, and all that comes from God is good. So all religions must be good, though sometimes seeming wrong.

A kiss, a bubble, or a prayer; a blow, reproof, or solemn scorn — are of religion. The plays of childhood, and the cheats of manhood, produced by human desires, are the fruits of religion. Great moral and worldly distinctions; material excellence and material degradation; sectarian convictions of excellence and goodness above those who are without the enclosure of a sect; fashionable extravagance and corresponding want; surfeiting and hunger; excessive indulgence and excessive restraint; bad actions and good actions — all these are the product of human desires, are the fruits of human religion. Human actions are produced by human desires; so all the doings of human life are the effect of religion, without a single exception.

Belief and doctrine have little to do with religion; *want* and *have* have more. There is no volition in belief; there is no volition in unbelief. Doctrine and belief are the smoke of our soul-desires, the worthless effects of religion. Every desire has a cause, and, consequently, is lawful. Every religion is of God, and, consequently, is good.

Every man and every woman is deeply and truly religious. And religion is a gift that comes, unseen, direct from the hand of nature. Who shall stand apart, and say, "*I am religious, and you, my brother, are not religious?*" Every belief is from the power of nature, and every desire is from the power of nature.

Fannie Green, who all church time thinks how handsome her new bonnet and dress look to others, is as truly religious as the excellent Mary who everybody knows to be pious and good, who listens to every word the minister says, and joins devotedly in prayer and praise.

The sportsman who shoots game and catches fish *on Sunday*, is no less religious than is the good minister who fires guns of self-righteousness at the faults of others, and fishes for men *on Sunday*. Both have desires that are true to the condition of each. Neither is in the pursuit of pain; one is not truer to life than the other; one loves happiness no more than the other.

The business man, who forms his plans and schemes for enterprises in commerce in sermon-time, is as true to God's religion as the man who hears every word of the sermon in the confidence of a certain hope that what he calls the word of God will be fulfilled; viz., "The wicked shall be turned into hell, and all the nations that forget God."

The man who laughs is as religious as the man who sighs.

Solemn, devotional, sectarian curses, are no more religious than unmeaning, trivial, secular curses.

The murder of restraint is no less the effect of religion than the murder of indulgence; both are the effect of human desire, and every human desire is natural religion.

The lady in heavy silk, in fine, clean linen, and neat kid gloves, has desires — is religious; she loves God; she loves happiness. And the woman in thin, dirty calico, in squalid wretchedness, in degradation, deep in sin, poor in spirit, is no less religious; desires happiness no less; loves God no less; has a heart that beats longing throbs for heaven no less than the other. Both are religious.

Religion ever brings its demands. Every desire must, in the order of its spiritual nature, be satisfied. The stream of Lethe washes away what the soul desires to lose, and the stream of God flows in to satisfy every want.

Nothing is heartily believed that is said by others,

unless it find a response from the soul-consciousness of the hearer.

A truth that relates to spiritual things can never be driven into a man from without. A capacity is developed in man for spiritual truths, or, what seems almost the same thing, truth is developed within and comes out of a man, as a rosebud unfolds its leaves and fragrance from within outward. Unseen spiritual streams of power flow into the soul, and the soul, from its own God-given nature, produces its own truths, as the bee produces honey by its own God-given nature.

No spiritual truth can be forced upon the soul by external teachings, no more than the fragrance of another flower can be forced into a rose, and substituted for its own peculiar fragrance.

There is no such thing as spiritual culture coming from the teachings of another.

A soul-conviction is the product of natural growth. A soul-conviction is a soul-truth — is a part of the soul. We hear a thought uttered by another; our souls respond, "How beautiful, how true is that thought!" The capacity for that truth, and, more, that truth itself, is already developed in our souls; and it may be that, by some undiscovered law, our souls have helped produce its utterance in the speaker. Other souls who hear the same thought responded to its utterance, "How silly — how false!" Those other souls have no capacity developed for that truth; they have not that truth developed yet. No man ever did, or ever can, interiorly accept religion from another man. Yet this may be done by pretence, and is, outwardly done; and such acceptance is changeable and fleeting, like other external things.

A creed may be offered to me for acceptance, and I may outwardly accept it; but my *soul* does not accept it, unless it is developed out of my soul; then its external presentation would be useless. Thus, to the soul of man, to that property of a man which is immortal, a creed, a belief, a doctrine, a religion, taught by another, is *nothing worth.* All religions, outwardly presented, outwardly taught, belong to outward things, not to the soul. All religions of this kind are good for material excellence, but for the soul are worthless. Such are the religions of which men take cognizance; such is the religion of our churches.

All outward, visible religions, all religions taught from books, from the pulpit, from the lips and pens of men and women, add nothing to the advancement of the soul heavenward, but tend to enhance the glory of material things. This seems right; for the soul grows just as fast, and no faster, while we polish matter, as it does while we disintegrate, break up, and destroy forms of material beauty. Our soul-desires, our heart-longings are just the same, let our hands do what they will, let our semblance be what it will, let our outward garments of religion be white, black, or any tinge or color, as they may chance to be.

Our soul-desires cannot be altered by external religion, but, in defiance of any and all outward influences, make perpetually *one eternal longing for happiness. This is religion* — religion, over which this outward world can have no influence. These desires are as much beyond our powers of control as was our birth — as is our immortality. They are the spontaneous productions of nature. Every desire is right, good, beautiful, true to the soul out of which it proceeds. And every truth, as it becomes a part of the soul's intelligence, is developed out of the soul itself, in which is sown the seeds of infinite knowledge, to germinate, grow, and unfold, in fragrance and beauty, forever and forever.

Seeds always germinate in darkness. So it is of the truths which germinate in the soul. In his own bosom man finds his God, immediate; his heaven or his hell, located.

The sun sometimes looks red, while it is the rising vapors of the earth that tinge its pure rays. The sun goes down, and night comes; it is the earth's own shadow that makes the darkness. The sun sends off its generous rays the same in our night time as it does in our day time. It is the earth itself, held in nature's hand, that makes the sun look red, and white, and black. So it is with the soul of man; its bloody vapors make a cloud, through which he sees a bloody God — a God of vengeance. The soul has revolutions; it has day and night. In the daytime, God is bright and beautiful; light is reflected from every object, for everywhere his rays of love are seen to fall. The night of the soul follows the day of the soul. In its revolution it turns its back to God, and in the shadow of itself it sees *no* God; God is darkness, God is black. It is in this natural darkness of the soul that a religion for its own salvation is conjured up. This is right. *Love*, which simply is desire, acts through all life, lives to death, and through death, and is then immortal. *Love is desire; desire is religion;* and there is not, there never was, a desire of the human soul that, to itself and in itself, was not *pure love.* Through matter, and the smoke and fumes of matter, these loves are often clouded, and appear impure *to sensuous* vision—to limited perception. From the great source of love uncounted streams flow out to human hearts, in channels made by a parent's impartial hand to all his own children. And when we shall see this spiritual influx, we shall see God's hand in every stream of love that flows to every human heart. Then we shall cease to say that the stream of God's love that flows to one heart, is better than the stream of God's love that flows to another heart; that one religion is better than another religion. Religion is human desire; and desire is love; and love is beyond the accidents of time, because it is immortal; and every love, in time, or after time, to our perception

"Will be as pure and white
As beams of shining light."

From the filth of refuse matter, or from the cleanest things of earth, it finally rises up to God, and mingles with the radiant beauties of celestial worlds. Religion is never gained by effort, struggle, force; but is a spontaneous production always developed in human desires.

SPIRITUALISM.

> "Now earth and heaven hold commune, day and night;
> There's not a wind but bears upon its wing
> The messages of God." * * *

It has been claimed that Spiritualism is simply a belief in the fact that spirits do communicate with mortals. This is but a superficial definition of the unmeasured reality that is hidden beneath the repulsive, outside mantle of Spiritualism, which mantle is material, and is seen only by material vision. This is not the definition of Spiritualism, and the development of ages may not define it, for Spiritualism is that which pertains to the soul and its immortality, and is as undefinable as is the progress of the soul.

The first recognition in Spiritualism is, the coming down of light to us. This comes of the teachings of the past. The idea that superior intelligences come to tell us something in words; that spirits do communicate — is but a reiteration, in a little more palpable form, of what the "religious" world has taught for ages. These teachings are external to the soul. Spiritual communications are in time and place. But Spiritualism has something deeper than this. It teaches that spirit fills all space; that it underlies and pervades all life and all matter, and that it tends upward forever; that knowledge does not come down, but that it comes up; it is the offspring of spirit-development; that knowledge is developed out of the germ of the soul, and is never received by the soul from without; that the soul holds within itself the germ of all knowledge it shall ever possess. The unfolding of this knowledge is ever under the immediate laws of nature, is developed by the unseen reality of spirit-power.

Spiritualism, in its truer definition, exhibits the conscious perception of realities like these, not seen; by the action of which, men in science and in ignorance, in wealth and in poverty, in sin and in holiness, in whatever place or condition, are moved on in the upward course of progression, independent of any effort or will of their own.

Spiritualism never came to any one by contact or contagion; if it did, it came and went. It comes spontaneously, springing up all over the earth the same, at the same time. Like an epidemic, it springs forth from every soul that has a condition developed for it. Spiritualists are made by nature, which is a stronger power than that of sectarian persuasion. Natural, spontaneous development is real; forced persuasion is a dark mist, through which the real can come up.

Shakspeare did not ask nature to make him what he was, but without a petition nature made him a Shakspeare. So it is of every man, great or little; and so it is of Spiritualism; it is nature's gift; it is nature's work; it has come unasked, uncalled for. There is no record in history of any religion that has ever sprung up simultaneously all over the earth, without leaders and promulgators, as Spiritualism has. Thus Spiritualism, as a religion, when compared with other religions, *is* something new, and, consequently, strange.

Spiritualism, like the God who gave it, is impartial. I know two bishops who are Spiritualists; I know ministers of all denominations who are Spiritualists; and a few deacons, and a great many church members. I know men who do not profess any religion, who are Spiritualists; I know infidels who are Spiritualists, and any quantity of sinners; I know sabbath-breakers, profane swearers, drunkards, gamblers, prostitutes, convicts, and rebels, who are Spiritualists. This gift of Heaven has come to all grades and classes, just as if God, in giving it, was perfectly regardless of the great distinctions that man has made between man and man.

The simple, foolish man has got it; the tattling old woman has got it; the lovely maiden has got it, and the intelligent matron, too; the honest laborer, and the man of tricks and stratagems; the recreant and the erring, the judicious and the just, have equal claims to its possession. It comes without respect of persons. In this respect it is new. *Real* Spiritualism costs no money; so the poor have it the same as the rich, and the rich have it the same as the poor. It comes forth from calico and rags, the same as from twilled silk and whole cloth; the town poorhouse that gives lodgings to forty families, the same as from the private mansion that gives lodgings to only one family, and cost ten times as much. It comes from the state prison just the same as from the church; from the peasant's garden, as much as from the consecrated altar. It comes on Monday the same as on Sunday.

"I don't believe it is true," says one, "for such wicked folks are Spiritualists! If it be of God, he would send it to his own children, to his Church, and only to his own people." In the light of Spiritualism, there are no children that are not God's children; there are no people that are not God's people; and if one child of God needs a gift from heaven more than another, it is the child of suffering and misery. The excellences of a virtuous life, when scanned, are only material; in real Spiritualism they are only the vapors of life. Polish matter forever, and it adds no polish to the spirit. What we call virtue, belongs to the material world — not the spiritual. Clean up and decorate the body, and make beautiful all its appurtenances, and it does nothing to the spirit in that body; elevate the body, and let all men bow in recognition to its elevation — it does not elevate the spirit. Tread down, wear, tear, and mutilate, even kill the body belonging to a human soul, and the spirit is untouched, uninfluenced.

We have been taught, substantially, that material excellence makes us spiritually excellent; a clean outside; just and upright walk before the world; a good example set to others by outside life and actions; an eternal war with what man calls evil impulses, planted by nature in our souls, will make our passport up to Heaven, and influence the world to reformation. Spiritualism, in the very manner of its coming, breaks the whole fabric of what has been called a *spiritual* superstructure, built on and made of material things, and scatters its fragments of fancies to the four winds of the earth. Spiritualism brings truth and enduring realities in its arms, and phantoms fade away before the light of its coming. These realities are felt, not seen, with physical eyes. It comes forth a spontaneous production of nature, the offspring of nature's inflexible laws; no human hand helps it; no human voice advances it; it is independent of the efforts, of the hands and the voices of men that have built and have supported churches, sects, and religions. There is not a shadow of sect or sectarianism about real Spiritualism; there is not, nor can there be, any human effort that can sustain it, or hold it up by the aid of even the smallest atom of power in the universe. Its currents flow *unseen* from the infinite ocean of spirit-life, into the souls of men and women, as they become developed for its reception by natural growth. As the river flows along a channel made by nature, moved by unchanging law, unbidden, ungoverned by man, so Spiritualism flows into the channel of the human soul that nature develops, and the manifestations of Spiritualism are the effect of this influx.

The fact that spirits do communicate, is but one of the effects of the real thing; it is not the definition of Spiritualism. Spiritualism, in its unseen beauty, is like the centrifugal and the centripetal forces of nature, that hold the starry worlds of immensity subservient to their silent power. The antagonism of one to the other makes the heavenly spheres move in circles and in silent harmony forever. These powers are unseen; we only know their effects. Spirit-power holds the intellectual universe by attraction and repulsion—by the centripetal and the centrifugal spirit-forces of nature—the same as worlds of matter are held and moved by these powers. The souls of men, in the circles of eternity, revolve upward forever. The recognition of real Spiritualism is the recognition of this spirit-power. The recognition of the fact that spirits do communicate, is only the recognition of one of the effects of this power, and conveys but the faintest idea of its reality.

One of the prominent features of Spiritualism is this: the finger of nature writes its tenets on each individual soul, for each individual soul. A Spiritualist learns no catechism, written in a book, and rehearses no creed that another has taught him. No Spiritualist ever goes to another Spiritualist for his soul convictions or his religious persuasion. In Spiritualism religious convictions flow from an unseen source into the soul, exactly in accordance with the nature of the soul, and proportionate to its capacities. All other religions have written creeds and rules of action, which are adopted for government.

You may say that the convention of Spiritualists at Plymouth adopted something of this sort in their published "Declaration of Sentiments." I affirm that Spiritualism did not do this, nor can it do any such thing. It was the "orthodoxy" of the convention that made this declaration, which savors so strongly of a religious creed, that it differs but little, if any, from other religious creeds. Spiritualism has no religious creed, nor can it ever have. The truly progressive soul has new convictions every day—so that the creed of yesterday would not answer for to-day.

Spiritualism recognizes *human souls;* and for the *government* of human souls, a power *unseen.* It cares but little for the soul's material habiliments, or its manifestations that the world sees, to *approve* or *condemn.* It heeds not the man-made garments of religious or moral beauty. The clean outside and the virtuous life are to Spiritualism just the same as the habiliments of crime, pollution, and degradation. These are each mortal; the soul is immortal.

In spirit-truth, the mephitic curse of pollution, of

prostitution, of drunkenness, of debauchery, pass away as the dews of morning when the sun rises. Spiritualism comes just the same to the self-debased and humiliated, as it does to the self-excellent and the self-righteous. Distinctions among men, to Spiritualism, are phantoms; and they fade away when Spiritualism comes, as the darkness of the morning does when the sun gets up.

The greatest wickednesses are but the damps of life, that are produced by soul-growth, and thereby soften and prepare the soul sooner for the development of new truth. Tears dissolve the cement of material love, and make bare the soul for the tendrils of spiritual love to cling to.

"Why don't Spiritualism, if true, come to the Church?" says one, and reiterate a thousand others. Because material love is there, woven into a beautiful, strong garment of self-excellence, which covers the soul when weak for protection. When Spiritualism does come there, every shred of this garment will be rent and scattered; for the soul shall then have grown to a strength where it needs such covering no longer.

"What!" says another, "do you mean to say that a person who has lived a truly religious life, has always been happy in the love of Christ and God, has ever been faithful and true to the teachings of the Bible and the church, is no more prepared to receive truth from the spirit-world, than is a prostitute, a drunkard, a rebel, a criminal?"

I do mean to say precisely this. I will tell you why I say that the last shall be first, and the first last. Whom the Lord loveth he chasteneth. Afflictions always benefit the soul's freedom; joy is only recreation, not the work of the soul's growth. Death of material love is the reward of sin, which is the effect of spiritual development. Self-approvement is the enjoyment of what is already possessed, not the cause which brings new possessions.

Every pain of woe and tear of anguish is a pulsation in the soul's progression. These are always the direct or indirect effect of what we call wickedness existing in the world somewhere. Who suffers more than the wretched sinner? Who suffers less than the good and faithful Christian, who chooses and walks in the way of pleasantness, where all the paths are *paths* of peace?

All the steps of human progress in the upward flight of every soul must be passed. Every degree of growth in the unfolding of the germ of the soul by the stern demand of God's laws must be passed. If hell be anywhere, and have existence, it must be on the lower steps of human progress; and every soul, to gain a higher ascent, must first pass over the steps below. Can another soul pass the ordeal of my affliction for me? No, never! There has never been a pang of human woe, that shall not be virtually mine in my progression. There is no degradation, no misery, no suffering, which I must not in my progression gain mastery over; and to do this, the misery and the suffering must be mine in sympathy, or in some form of suffering. There is no squalid wretchedness of earth that I need turn aside from, for it is mine, or shall be mine in spirit. We triumph over misery, never, before we have the power to do so, which power only comes of its possession.

> "There is no true knowledge till descent,
> Nor then, till after."

Hell shall sometime rise on wings of ecstacy to praise God forever, and Spiritualism tells me that when this shall be, I shall go to heaven too.

Spiritualism is the first and the only religion on earth that exists independent of extraneous influences; that goes back to spirit to find the causes of *all* human actions; that deals with spirit independent of matter. Spiritualism has to do, or will have, with unseen causes, not with visible effects; it reaches beyond the effects, which we see manifest in the material world, and recognizes the real thing, which is spirit, and which is far more powerful, more lovely, more enduring than all the powers, the beauties, and the glories of the material world. Spiritualism asks for and wants no material organization for its support. It asks for no house in which to worship God, for everywhere the soul is in the house of God. It asks for no creed which human reason fabrics to bind itself unto, by sectarian chains that, in reality, hold nobody. It asks for no printed book to guide the soul to heaven, for the soul feels the love of angels drawing it upward and homeward. It asks for no external teachings to prepare the soul for heaven, for in it the soul feels and recognizes the unseen power of God in every act of life, working out its inevitable, beautiful destiny, and preparing it for the joys of heaven.

THE SOUL, ONLY, IS REAL.

The soul is our governor, our teacher, and our guide, in all that pertains to spirit-life. Human reason is only its agent in matter. The soul, and that which sustains it, is all there is of human existence that endures. And we have no real conscious recognition of the soul's existence until intuition is developed in us. When this comes, the perceptions of the soul run through all matter, as lightning runs through air, and the world of causes is clear to its perceptions; it sees, then, the now unseen laws of all things. And sooner or later all the forms of the material world disintegrate and dissolve by the rising up of the spirit, which is to be recognized as the living reality.

All life that is spiritual is immortal. Spirit is the basis of all life, and can never, *never* die. All that is material, or that pertains to the material, is the effect of the spirit and is changeable.

From whence the spirit cometh, and whither it goeth in its eternal destiny, we cannot tell, save by the light of intuition, which is yet but feebly developed in any human soul on earth. All that we know of the soul, which is scarcely any thing yet, is alone from the light of intuition. All of life that we have taken cognizance of yet in our earthly existence, save the spirit, is but the shadows of matter that in the light of the spirit will pass away. The soul and its appurtenances are the only real things of human existence.

Every deed of human life is subservient to the soul. Our desires are servants of the soul; our will is the agent of our desires, and our deeds are the products of our will. The soul is the great moving cause of all our actions. And still behind the soul our intuitions shall discover other causes; and then perhaps still further find causes of causes, and on, still on, *ad infinitum;* and then exclaim, O God! what realms of hidden causes lie beyond the reach of our developments, which the soul in its eternal progress shall never cease to find! New, still new, forever!

The soul of man! What immensity, what illimitable grandeur is in the word! How small, how finite are the mightiest conceptions of the soul's vision now, when compared with the illimitable grandeur of its undefined, eternal progression in truth and light.

SELF-RIGHTEOUSNESS.

A consciousness of evil is simply, in one word, a proclamation of "*your faults*" and "*my virtues.*" This is popular orthodoxy. If there be any one thing that seems puerile and ridiculous — that seems like an old garment no longer useful and necessary — it is the idea, that for ages has been so fondly cherished; viz., *that one child of God is better than another child of God; that one immortal soul is better than another immortal soul; that one is more evil and another is less evil; that, in our spiritual existence, one is higher and another is lower.*

Humanity moves heavenward together, — all men and all women in one solid phalanx on the journey of unending progress. All sail on one level sea of life along together, in storms and in sunshine, over the waves of progress. No one is above — no one is below. A wave may bear *you* a little higher, for a moment, than *others*, but *you* descend again while *others* come up — and the average level is the fixed destiny of each one. All sail on the great sea of God, whose hand holds both the winds and the waves, and whose infinite love directs us as we sail.

I cannot but conclude that the element in humanity that has made distinctions of good and bad, high and low, in the souls of men,— I mean the element of self-righteousness, — will sometime find its culminating point, and, like fruit matured to ripened rottenness, drop off and go back again to the earth that has given it a life and existence of tremendous vigor; and our spiritual eyes will be opened to the more real and enduring truth of a spiritual oneness; of a universal brotherhood; of a loving household of human beings, whose father is God; whose interests are *one;* whose home is a heaven of harmony, peace, love, and kindness — *not a heaven of distinctions.*

The whole idea of evil, which is always in others, not in ourselves, has its beginning in, and its outgrowth from, selfishness, self-excellence, self-righteousness. But this selfishness is lawful to the condition that produces it — necessary in early spiritual growth.

I will make one affirmation which all men cannot disprove — it is this: The man who sees the most evil in the world, and is most troubled by its influences, and feels and utters the severest protests against its existence, — without one single exception, — possesses self-righteousness commensurate with the magnitude of the evil he sees.

Can a man consistently condemn a wrong deed, unless he conscientiously feels himself better than the man who commits that wrong deed? No. Men are sincere in a belief in hell — in the existence of evil; they are sincere, also, in the condemnation of evil; but the *cause* of a belief in evil, and of its condemnation, is a consciousness of self-excellence and self-righteousness.

"Our preachers first think they are safe."

He who thinks it is his solemn duty to work for the redemption of humanity from sin and evil deeds, *always* thinks it is *others*, not *himself*, that need redemption.

Devils, as we call them, are the immediate messengers of God, whose mission it is, by obsessions and "devilish deeds of injury," to relieve humanity sooner of the cumbersome, heavy chains of self-righteousness. The work of "devils," I cannot doubt, shall ultimate in the highest good for all human souls — shall blossom at last in the fruition of Infinite Love. But I do not think that "devils" can yet see the good that will come out of their deeds any more than we, who are not a whit their inferiors or their superiors, can see yet the good that shall blossom out of every deed that we do. God, in his infinite wisdom, sets us all at work, and keeps us at work; and every deed we do in life is done in wisdom, God being the witness. He *knows*, in light, that his own work is right, while men and devils in *darkness* swear it is not.

> "* * * all the world is but
> A quality of God, and * * *
> All the countless souls therein,
> The *best*, the *worst*, are heirs to one salvation."

I see a hand of wisdom in all the various influences of so-called evil spirits. And of influences called evil by others, sincerely, without any qualification by the use of the words *positive*, *accidental*, *real*, and *comparative*, I solemnly affirm, in plain English, I know no evil, no wrong. I use the word evil because others use it; I use it to convey an idea that is hard to convey without its use. All evil influences are means, or effects of means, to work out the highest good. So that which is, or is to be, productive of good, I cannot call wrong or evil. When a consciousness of evil shall cease to exist, self-righteousness has gone where darkness goes when light comes; has gone to a local hell of fire and brimstone, where nothing exists.

SELF-EXCELLENCE.

"Very boastful was Iagoo;
Never heard he an adventure,
But himself had met a greater;
Never any deed of daring,
But himself had done a bolder:
Never any marvellous story,
But himself could tell a stranger.
No one ever shot an arrow
Half so far and high as he had;
Ever caught so many fishes,
Ever killed so many reindeer,
Ever trapped so many beaver.
None could run so fast as he could,
None could dive as deep as he could,
None had made so many journeys,
None had seen so many wonders,
As this wonderful Iagoo."

There is this element of self-excellence in humanity. All possess it; some in a greater, some in a less, degree. Some think it and feel it without expressing it in words; while others are free to express it without disguise.

No scholar was ever so learned that another scholar did not think himself more learned. No statesman was ever so great that another did not think himself a greater. No man was ever so religious that another did not think himself more religious. No man ever took a step in reform that another man did not claim to have taken before him. No man ever sent forth a fresh thought, an original idea, that another man did not claim the credit of. No Spiritualist ever had an angel guardian so pure that another did not claim a purer.

This element is well developed in human souls; I should think that it had reached its culminating point. The fruit of self-excellence is ripe. Walt Whitman said: "There was more in trivialities, in vulgar persons, in slaves, dwarfs, weeds, rejected refuse, than I had supposed." And I have often thought that there may be something in the development of this ridiculous self-excellence, now so ripe and big in humanity, more than we have supposed. To sensuous perception it is truly repulsive and disgusting; but in spirit it may be otherwise. Festus says that the weakest things are to be made examples of God's might. It may be so with this apparent weakness of human nature.

Man esteems himself almost a god, and in this estimation there may be a godlike element. I know one lady who sincerely believes in a personal God, and that God is specially her guardian spirit. I know another lady who sincerely believes that she is constantly influenced and especially guarded by the spirit of Jesus Christ. And we Spiritualists are exceedingly prone to believe that we are guarded by very high spirits; by those who were high in the material world. A great many times I have heard Spiritualists say, "Oh! dark spirits never come to *me;* only pure and good spirits come to influence *me*, or communicate with *me*. I never associate with that class of Spiritualists that draw around them dark spirits." Obsessions have regulated and levelled up these cases, or will do it. A great many Spiritualists, by letters and by conversation, have signified a positive belief that they had, individually, a mission to perform that was not a whit inferior to that of Christ. A multitude have fondly cherished this belief; some silently, but earnestly; others openly, and with a wild fanaticism. With some it has lasted a few months; with others, a year, or two, or three. It is the greatest medicine for self-humiliation in the whole spiritual pharmacopia. By this means a man loses his self-righteousnes and his self-excellence. By disappointment in the fondest and most ardent longings for material glory, he is thrown down upon the level plain of humanity where the cross of Christ stands. Perhaps no other means could have brought him there so soon.

How futile, how childlike appears this love of exultation of one above another! How fictitious and how fleeting appears the reality! How beautiful is humanity! How sweet is the concord and oneness of a human brotherhood! Christ was meek and lowly; the inhabitants of celestial worlds feel no such self-excellence as this wonderful Iagoo felt. But this self-excellent manifestation is in its place, is right.

VISION OF MRS. J. S. ADAMS.

"I SEE all the children of creation standing in ranks, irrespective of grades or worlds. I see them in space; and every soul has its spaceway filled by a spirit above, and that by an attendant; and on and on they reach, into space illimitable. They seem like pyramids of life, towers of animation. There are some beneath thee; there are many above thee. The soul that stands beside thee has them all the same; and thus they seem like millions on millions of chains, going up to immortality, to Deity. And each soul seems a link fastened in by God's own hand, and riveted by time. He stretches forth his hand to take one link, and it draws the chain to himself. And I gaze far, far into celestial courts, till my vision fails, till brilliancy repels, and I draw back. Then down I look, far beneath the human chain, into matter undeveloped, till vision fails me here, and I draw back amazed.

"We, too, are linked together in one chain of this existence. Thy existence is riveted into mine, and mine links on another's, and another link fastens itself to thee. We move on with the throng, and the links of none are unprotected. There is no desert heart; there is no forsaken child."

HUMAN DISTINCTIONS.

The comparisons we make between man and man belong to the material world, not to the spiritual; the distinctions of human life are ephemeral, not enduring.

"—— merit or demerit none I know."

Could we see all men with the eye of Omniscient Wisdom, I cannot doubt that we should fail to find in the whole man any merit or demerit; any distinction which would make one more excellent than another. We see not, nor do we comprehend, the vast amount of beauty that is budding and growing in *every* immortal soul. We judge of men by external, isolated characteristics; and thus we consecrate in the man we call excellent a vast amount of *nothingness;* while in the man we call evil we condemn a vast amount of *real goodness.* We judge men when we do not know them; the interior man we cannot see or know; and if we judge a man, we judge him always by a material standard, without knowledge of his spiritual worth.

One man has developments in one direction, another man in another direction. One man in his external developments is excessively good, while in his internal developments of goodness he may appear to be wanting. Another has external developments of great apparent evil, and large unseen, unspoken developments of great goodness.

The various external manifestations of human life

are not a true index of the character of the soul. By these manifestations we can no more judge of the condition and quality of the soul than we can judge of the gold in the refiner's fire by the smoke that ascends upward from the burning dross.

Could we weigh each man in the scales of eternal truth, no one who has an immortal soul made by God and growing up to him, would in any possible degree be found wanting; neither would one soul be found to possess more value, more weight in goodness, than another.

We talk of the *family of humanity*, of a *universal brotherhood.* In a universal brotherhood am I better than my brother, or is my brother better than I am? Are there distinctions in the household of humanity? Are not all equal?

All distinctions made between the souls of men are like an *ignis fatuus*, and will vanish from their minds with other delusions. A God *impotent*, *feeble*, *and angry*, and a devil *all-powerful*, subtle, cunning, and triumphant, these are kindred delusions, and will fade away and be buried in one grave, to be known and seen no more in a higher condition of human growth.

Last January the heart of that poor little beggar girl beat beneath the thin covering of calico, as *sensibly* to the treatment of cruelty or kindness, as did the heart of the child of fortune beneath warm clothing, and furs of fitch or sable. Each one of these little girls was governed by the same eternal laws. The despised poor and the courted rich have the same claims on the laws of nature, — on the laws of love. The Duke of Richmond, with his home and farm of thirty-five square miles, in crowded England, which farm is covered with every thing material love can ask for, and an income of $800,000 a year, is governed by the same unerring, undeviating laws that poor Patrick is, who shovels up the grades of our railroads for a dollar and a quarter a day. The laws of birth, of life, of death, are common to each; the laws of God, through nature, govern both; destiny holds one, and destiny holds the other, too, in her eternal grasp. God is impartial — destiny has no monopolies. Air is everywhere; it is not theft to breathe it. All that pertains to the spirit is free; what to one is free in spirit, to all is.

Material monopolies are monopolies of fiction; the laws of nature level them. Every sinner had birth pretty much after the same manner that every saint had. Trace a sinner and a saint along together from infancy to old age, and it will be found that the laws of nature govern both about the same; the law of gravitation holds each alike to the earth; an earthquake would swallow one the same as the other; when it rains, it rains for both the same; the sun shines for both; water quenches thirst and food satisfies hunger the same in each; each have necessities to be answered, which do not differ. The saint has two hundred and fifty bones in his body, and so has the sinner; cut off the femoral artery, and either would bleed to death in fifteen minutes. Tubercles in the lungs will ulcerate, *cætera paribus*, about alike in both. Each has consciousness and intelligence, has love and hate, good and bad; nature chains each; destiny holds each. Where, in nature, shall we look for that mighty difference between the good and the bad man? Nature points no finger to it; and nature is the purest revelation from the hand of God. This great distinction between good and bad men is a moral and religious fiction, found nowhere except in the vapor of man's belief, in his materialism, in man's judgment. It is not a reality that endures, but with the other changing, fleeting things of time, falls away from before the soul's vision, and, like clouds that were, are gone, leaving not a trace behind.

EXTREMES ARE BALANCED BY EXTREMES.

"In changing moon, in tidal wave,
Glows the feud of *Want* and *Have*."

Whenever we see *excess* in life, then we may be sure there is somewhere a *want*, corresponding to the amount of excess. If there is extravagance and waste of necessary and useful things, there must be somewhere in humanity a corresponding need unanswered. Where the tide of earthly riches runs high in one place, it is correspondingly low in another.

A woman in Chicago recently bought a shawl, for which she paid one thousand dollars; and a set of lace, for which she paid five hundred dollars. Another woman in New York was recently arrested for stealing a turkey. The officer who arrested her and "*redeemed*" the stolen turkey, reported to the judge who was to try her case, that there was not a vestige of food in her attic room, which room was destitute of every comfort; and that her three children, before he made the arrest, were so hungry that they had torn the raw meat off from the turkey's legs and wings, and had eaten it. The judge thought that the Bible justified stealing to satisfy hunger, and let the poor woman go. And perhaps she is hungry still, to balance some other excess.

Fifteen hundred dollars, the amount paid for the shawl and laces, if judiciously expended on the soil of some of the millions of uncultivated acres of land in our country, would produce one thousand bushels of wheat and five hundred turkeys, or an amount of produce large enough to feed a great many poor widows, with their starving families, for the whole winter.

Anna West had a Christmas present sent to her — a box of jewellery worth eleven hundred dollars. Mary Jones did not have a present; and was so poor that she could not go to church, because she had not even the plainest clothes to wear. Mary worked hard for a dollar and a half a week, and with all that she earned she could hardly make her aged father and mother comfortable. Extremes are balanced by extremes.

A woman in Cincinnati came so near starvation, that she sold her baby for five dollars, whereby she was enabled to procure food to sustain life. A gentleman on Colonnade Row, in Boston, the same week, had served on his Christmas dinner-table fourteen luxuriant courses, with eleven servants in attendance; this excess was balanced by a corresponding want.

Jeanette Follett, at New Year's evening ball, wore a dress made of white tarleton, with twenty-four flounces edged with a full ruche of tulle illusion, and the ruche itself edged with very narrow black lace. Over this, she wore a berthe to match the flounces, composed of four chrysanthemums — pink, pale lilac, white and light cerese without leaves. Bouquets to match the skirt, six on each side, arranged *en tablier*, from the bottom of the skirt to the waist. Her hair was dressed with chrysanthemums and lilacs, and black and white blonde. On the same day little Mary Mahoney — in a dirty, ragged calico dress, an old rag for a shawl, hugged close over her shoulders; with an old pair of cast-off shoes twice as large as her little feet, and holes in them, through which her naked, freezing toes could be seen; she was without drawers and other under-clothes, shivering with the winter's cold — asked alms, because her father and mother were hungry. Her father was poor and helpless with disease, and her mother was dying with consumption. With shrinking reluctance she said, "*Please give me a cent to buy some bread!*"

Jeanette had every earthly comfort in her possession, and she had a great deal more than was necessary — while little Mary was destitute of almost every necessary earthly comfort. Jeanette was smiled upon, bowed to, praised, and flattered. Mary was frowned upon, sent away, chilled and almost frozen for want of human sympathy and human compassion. Is Jeanette better than Mary? No; each one is a lawful child of God. If Jeanette claims more of the good things of this world than is necessary for her, there must be a deficiency somewhere — and by fate it has fallen on Mary. Mary only needs that which Jeanette does not need for her comfort. Give to Mary what Jeanette does not need for her comfort and happiness, and Mary, and her father, and mother, too, would be made comfortable. Nature will always balance extremes by extremes.

But nature's God fails not to take care of *little things and desolate, rejected little girls.* Little Mary will find rest in heaven sooner for her sufferings. Her suffering is good for her — it draws her love earlier to the realities of the spiritual world. Mary will some time see that it is the hand of Wisdom that has produced her suffering for her more rapid growth in goodness, and be thankful that she has suffered. So it will be with all those who suffer from deprivation and want, and also from any other earthly cause. God in nature takes care of us for our good, always.

THE TIES OF SYMPATHY.

ALL human beings are bound together by ties of sympathy, which our earthly perceptions cannot recog nize and eternity will not sever. One unseen pulse of sympathy throbs in all humanity. The sufferings of those who are bound in the prison-house, influence all who are not in the prison-house; the horrors of war influence all; the crimes of a few are felt by many; the afflictions of one are felt by all; the pains of one are the pains of millions; my suffering is your suffering, and your suffering is my suffering; the unseen power of sympathy runs everywhere, where human life is, and no joy or sorrow exists anywhere, that does not reach throughout the domain of all human existence. This mighty power of sympathy is yet unrecognized, and cannot be recognized by outward perception; soul-perception alone will recognize it, see it, feel it, and know it.

We are all God's children, all members of the same household, all bound together by ties that make one great human family. We all came from the same Great First Cause, and are all destined for the same eternal home. We have all nestled in the arms of a mother's love, and played in innocent childhood. We have grown to years of responsibility, and have been set adrift upon the world to act our part. Circumstance and condition—I had almost said fate—have disposed of us. One in early life is made food for worms; another by accident is crippled for the remainder of his *earthly* life; another is for many years stretched upon a bed of sickness; one is rich; another is poor. One is flattered, courted, and loved; another is an outcast, degraded and scorned; one is a criminal, and another thanks God that he is not the same; one lives in tears, another in sunshine; one is intelligent, another is ignorant; one is a publican, and one a pharisee; one judges, another is judged; one condemns, another is condemned; one is master, another is servant; one rules, another is ruled; the life of one is spent in constant toil, while another spends a life of ease and repose; one eats the plainest food, and, for want of even that, suffers from hunger, while another is surfeited with the richest, costliest food, with luxuries in abundance; one is a beggar, another is a miser; one is ragged, another is clad in fine linen and costly silks; one is in prison, while another is in freedom. And such, and such are the varied conditions of human life in matter. And all souls in these various walks of life — no matter where they are, or what they are — are watched over and taken care of by the same eye that numbers the hairs of our heads. Each soul is a flower in the garden of eternal life, that is cared for and shall be clothed in beauty with more beneficent kindness of our Father, than are the lilies of the field.

By Infinite Wisdom all the various conditions of joy and sorrow existing in all, are, by the power of sympathy, made the property of all.

ALL MEN ARE IMMORTAL.

It is claimed by some that *no* human soul is immortal; it is claimed by others that *some, not all* human souls, are immortal; it is claimed and declared by multitudes, that *all* human souls are immortal. The last claim is in harmony with the deepest desires and the holiest longings of every human being. The immortality of no soul can be proved by any philosophy that belongs to earth. The evidence of immortality — the only positive, incontrovertible evidence is in the soul's intuition, which intuition for a time is wisely concealed in the soul's desires. In the desire for immortality alone may we seek *and find* the evidence, the sure and positive evidence of its reality, and everybody has this evidence of immortality in that desire.

No human soul desires to lose its identity ever; desires any thing short of an immortal existence. A denial, or a fractional denial, of the immortality of the living souls that make up humanity belongs not to intuition, but is repulsive to the sweetest, the deepest, the holiest desires of everybody's intuition; it belongs to the philosophies of earth; to the orthodoxy of self-righteousness.

There is room enough in the limitless area of creation for all life to exist, to progress, and increase in beauty forever and forever.

If *any life* is immortal, *all life* is immortal. The philosophy of earth may call this assumption; but if it does, what matters it? Intuition transcends the facts of all philosophies. Philosophies belong not to the soul's intuitions; they are only effects.

The life of every leaf, on every forest tree that ever grew, still lives, and will live forever. The life of every flower that ever bloomed on earth still lives in real spiritual existence, and will live forever. The life of every insect and every reptile can never die, but must hold each its place in life forever. All animal and vegetable existence that has ever lived, lives still, and must live forever, because life can never die.

When life goes out of matter, we say that death has come. Death is only the separation of life from matter. Little Hiawatha saw the rainbow in the heavens, and asked the wrinkled, old Nokomis, who nursed his childhood,—

> "* * * What is that Nokomis?
> And the good Nokomis answered:
> 'Tis the heaven of flowers you see there;
> All the wild flowers of the forest,
> All the lilies of the prairie,
> When on earth they fade and perish,
> Blossom in that heaven above us."

All life in the vegetable creation rises up forever, with ever-increasing beauties, and all life in the animal creation must do the same; so if all life is immortal, both in the vegetable and in the animal kingdoms, the life of *all men* must be immortal too.

All matter is pregnant with the elements of eternal life; life that becomes manifest in creation, in forms that are infinite in variety. So it is not necessary for the production of human life, that we call the highest life, to absorb the identity of forms of life that we call lower. My intuition repels the thought that my life is made up of the sacrificed identities of countless forms of lower life. Creation has infinite beauty, and infinite variety constitutes this infinite beauty, and must, in order to support this variety, exist forever.

All life that we have cognizance of, is but spirit reaching out through matter, and all spirit is immortal. It is spirit, it is life that produces all matter, and all the various forms of matter — and matter, like old scales, fall off from the real life, and this falling off is all that death is. No matter can in any possible way affect any life, for life is spirit brought to light in the material world. Sensuous vision by the aid of matter sees not life, but only the effects of life.

To draw a line between crazy men, and men that are not crazy; between foolish men, and men that are not foolish; between idiotic men, and men that are not idiotic; between men that are bad, and men that are not bad; between men that are well organized, and men that are not well organized; between men that are matured and ripened, and men that are not matured and ripened; between the *buds* and the *blossoms* of human souls, and say that on one side of this line is immortality and eternal identity, and on the other side is non-immortality and but a temporary identity — I say to do this, is to trace an unreal line in darkness, which is as futile and as "orthodox" as the conceptions of a hell that is to torment God's own dear children in unutterable agony forever. This idea belongs to the trash deduced from human philosophies, all of which trash with its philosophies will be, in the soul's advancement, consigned to nonentity and non-immortality by the overpowering development of intuition.

In the desires, in the longings of every soul, exist

budding intuition, that shall grow up and rise triumphant over earth and its philosophies, over hell and its damnation, over nonentity and all non-immortality.

The basis of a consciousness of immortality sleeps in the longings and in the desires of human souls, and here also is found the only sure and indestructible basis of Spiritualism. All men and all women possess the means that shall develop the conscious evidence of immortality, and to all, without any exception, the means shall be consciously available.

"* * * Human souls
Have diverse forms and features;
All are lovely; different offices and strengths;
Powers, orders, tendencies; * * *
Different glories and delights, are all immortal.
* * Perfect from God they came,
And in holy exellences have various beauties.
God's love shall lift them all to heaven."

THERE ARE NO EVIL SPIRITS.

BROADLY and unreservedly I do declare that I know nothing of the existence of evil spirits anywhere in God's creation. All spirits are good, because immortal. A soul, though buried in the densest darkness of human woe, has God within; has in its nature seeds of eternal life; of infinite progression; of angel beauty; of celestial holiness. Shall a baby be called "*evil*" because it is not born a man? Shall a spirit be called "*evil*" because it begins low in the scale of human progress, and *necessarily* in darkness treads upon the lower rounds of the ladder of eternal progress *first*, as God has wisely ordered?

Do not fear "evil" spirits, my friends. I tell you, as a truth of God that cannot be disproved by man, that no spirit *will*, or CAN, come to us, to influence us, that is beneath ourselves; that is "*wickeder*" than we are. We may as well, and better, be afraid of ourselves.

We have already seen enough of spirit, to know that attraction is the governing power of spiritual existence. Like seeks like in the great spiritual universe of God, forever.

Would we drive an "evil" spirit away that ruffles the waters of our external life? We may as well attempt to banish the deepest longings of our souls from our existence.

The "evil" that we see in the things around us, in spirits, is but the reflection of ourselves in the mirror of creation. We are always pretty good ourselves — or think we are. Antagonism, enmity, evil intents and purposes we see manifested in so-called evil spirits, is but the shadow of ourselves. If we have not learned this fact, we shall surely find it in a future lesson of our spiritual education. And when this fact becomes a part of our intelligence, we may bid farewell to all the fear we have of evil spirits.

We have so much confidence in our own goodness, that when we learn that the evil in the world is but the real character of ourselves reflected, we shall cease to believe in its existence. A very susceptible clairvoyant said to me, a few months since: —

"I see an innumerable host of devils around you. Why, they frighten me! As far as my spirit-eyes can reach through yonder interminable avenue, filled in perfect order, I see hosts on hosts, legions on legions of devils, of evil spirits. Every one of them has an eye fixed on you. Why, what are they going to do with you? They will surely destroy you! Hold a moment! I see their intentions. They all look kindly and pleasantly upon you. I can now read their hearts. Every one is your friend. They only wait your bidding. They will do you any thing you ask them to do. They are kind to you, and ever will be, because you are not opposed to them, and never can be. I cannot see existing in your soul an effort to resist one of them; but you are kind to them, and this kindness overcomes what at first seemed to me evil in them; and in their natures I can see an unmeasured willingness, and a power, too, for the accomplishment of the mightiest purposes for human good. I cannot now see an evil design or desire in one of them. How mighty for good shall this almost infinite host of beings be! As I *now* see them, they are good — they are all beautiful. Hold again; I now discover that these legions before me are exactly like the spirits of men and women who now live on earth, and it is only my own vision that first made them look so dark and devilish. How beautiful each one now appears to me!"

I must confess that I have just as much confidence in these spirits, who appear as they are, as I have in the spirits who make loud proclamations about being very high up in the spheres. I have known spirits who belonged to the "seventh sphere," get very angry when their *highness* was doubted. Touch the dignity of any high spirit (I mean professedly high), in the form or out of it, and the spirit loses his temper.

I have seen many spiritual realities, in visions, so called (doubt it, if you please — it matters not), and if there be such a thing as *high* in spiritual things, the *highest* is the *humblest*— the *highest* is the *lowest;* and I am forced to the conclusion that the words, "the high," and "the low," "the evil," and "the good," as applied to infant human souls on earth, and to their guardian spirits, are *the veriest phantoms of spiritual infancy*, that must fade away in the light of maturer spiritual growth.

There is a great deal of common sense in these obsessing "devils," as they are called. They have dropped the airs of self-righteousness themselves, and are making others do the same. They are better educated in spiritual things than the man is who feels holy himself, and says, "In the name of God I command you devils to depart."

According to my experience with men, I have been able to draw ten times as much real benevolence, real kindness, and real goodness, from the practical lives of men who were called "devilish bad," as I have from men who believed that they were almost as good as Christ. But I doubt not that one is as good as the other. I fail to find in practical, every-day life, merit in one balanced by demerit in another; good in one balanced by bad in another. All are good; *the spirits that guard and influence men are always like the men they influence.*

Evil is a phantom always to be rendered in the first person and singular number, but always is rendered, by those who see it, in the second or third person and plural number.

What you call evil spirits, all men kneel to and swear they don't. Evil spirits — according to your definition of evil spirits — move the world and hold humanity. Lucifer says: —

> "Have I not all the honor of the earth?"

Would you touch a spring to advance human progress, speak, a *friend in soul*, to the army of a legion of devils, as you please to call them, utter the mandate with feelings *en rapport* with the love that emanated from the soul of Christ, and, simultaneously with the going forth of the mandate, the work is done. Lucifer has proposed the following plan of salvation: —

> "Wait till * * * * *
> Some angel comes and stirs *your* stagnant souls,
> Then plunge into *yourselves* and rise redeemed."

There are no evil spirits that come to influence us. Spirits like ourselves come and influence us for our good always, and they are never worse than we are, and we are always as good as we can be for the time we have existed.

HARMONY OF SOUL THAT THE ALL-RIGHT DOCTRINE PRODUCES.

"Bring out your balance ; get in man by man ;
Add earth, heaven, hell, the universe ; that's all.
God puts his finger in the other scale,
And up we bounce a bubble. * * *"

'The world is perfect as concerns itself,
* * O'er the meanest atom God reigns
Omnipotent, as o'er the universe."

"We are imbecile, * * * * *
We see dark sides of things — *sometime* there *must be* light."

Without *any* feeling of antagonism to views that may seem opposed to the views of this book, from the most sincere convictions of my soul, I affirm, that what we call sin and evil in human actions, *is a necessity*, and, being a necessity, it is lawful and right. The views of Horace Seaver, William Loyd Garrison, Ralph Waldo Emerson, Theodore Parker, Henry Ward Beecher, Spurgeon, E. H. Chapin, A. L. Stone, and Nehemiah Adams, and all doctrines, creeds, and opinions, all over the world, this book accepts as being true to the conditions that produce them.

This subject is as vast as the universe ; it is as unmeasured as infinitude. A clear view of this question of infinite good, covers all the beauty, a thousand times told, that the wildest imagination can conceive. It is in perfect harmony with the beautiful teachings of Christ, and all that is good and holy in the Church and in all religions. It accepts every creed as being necessary to the condition that produced it. It is a platform on which all other platforms rest. It is a circle in which all other circles exist. It is in harmony with all evil; it sees all that is wrong and repulsive to the soul's higher longings, as being the effect of a means in the ordering of Divine Wisdom, for the production of the greatest possible good for humanity. It sees God in all his works ever manifest, replete in power and wisdom. It sees all the manifestations of life, both good and bad, as being the immediate effect of nature's laws — laws that were never broken, and never can be. It recognizes the latent germ of crime as meaning and potent as crime developed; and the latent germ of goodness as powerful and weighty as goodness developed. It recognizes the elements of good and evil, in a low condition of human progress, as being inseparably blended, necessary and inevitable. It sees the manifestations of every human soul, whether good or bad, as being the necessary result of a certain condition, in which condition is to be found a natural cause that produced the good or bad action. It sees that,

> "* * * The weakest things
> Are to be made examples of God's might;
> The most defective, of his perfect grace."

All ill, all woe, all curses, are only clouds that necessarily rise up and pass away, and

> "Every thing seems good and lovely and immortal;
> The whole is beautiful; and I can see
> Naught wrong in man nor nature, naught not meant.
> The world is but a revelation. All things
> Are God, or of God."

Judas, the traitor, was as faithful to the condition of his being as was St. John, the divine — each performed the mission assigned to teach, lawfully and truly. The lowest brick fills its place, and is useful in the wall of ten thousand other bricks, just the same as the highest brick that caps the superstructure. In the architecture of God's great universe each human soul fills its place as designed by the builder. Every human soul is as a brick — no more, no less — in the mighty superstructure of the temple of Deity.

Behind the holy deeds of Fenelon there existed natural causes that produced them; he could not help the manifestations of good. Behind the dark deeds of King Herod, the enemy of Christ, there existed natural causes that produced the wicked deeds of his life; he could not help so doing. In Fenelon there is no merit; in Herod there is no demerit. God created both, and the laws of God governed both, one no less than the other; each were true to the conditions of the life they lived; there were causes existing, in each, for the deeds which each committed, which causes were in nature, were God's causes. So there is no laudation for Fenelon, and no condemnation for Herod; there is no comparison made between the two; no judgment to be instituted. Fenelon is the child of God; Herod is the same; each an heir of eternal life, and the blessings of God, that await them in the coming future. Fenelon is no nearer God than Herod is, for God is everywhere, and his laws govern every thing.

That woman of shame and suffering that met Christ at Jacob's well, was just as near God before she preached Christ as she was after. The sufferings consequent upon her sins had prepared her soul to blossom in humility, and send forth its fragrance in the love of Christ to humanity. She was the first preacher of the gospel of Christ, and she was a prostitute.

I cannot say to the wretched sinner, to the rebel, to the criminal of darkest deeds, to the inebriate, the sensualist, the prostitute, the financier, or to the holy man — come with me and seek salvation; each and all are held in the hand of infinite *Wisdom*, *Love*, and *Power*, and so am I; no one more, and no one less than another. There is no philosophy to be found in the doctrine of universal salvation, except it be in the all-right doctrine.

Do the noblest desires of the soul want anybody to be unhappy forever? No. All hell fades out of view, as the phantom of a dream, when the soul can see that all that God has made is right.

The cup of bitterness we must drink as Christ did; we cannot keep it from our lips; it is our Father's will that we should drink it, and our Christ's example; it is for our good; it is our passport to heaven.

Your opinion, your creed is right to your soul, whatever it may be; it is the lawful effect of the condition of your soul; it could not be otherwise with causes existing there. Here is a doctrine that accepts not only opinions and creeds, but every deed of goodness and every deed of evil, as being necessary and right, that ever existed in the great family of humanity. It involves the elements of infinite forgiveness, of humility, which holds the soul on one level human brotherhood. It is in these views we catch glimpses of the dawning of that day, when "the wilderness and the solitary place shall be glad; the desert shall rejoice and blossom as the rose, and all shall see the glory of the Lord, the excellency of our God." "The wayfaring man though a fool, shall not err in the way of holiness."

Take all the teachings of the past in which the infinitude of God's power, wisdom, and love has been taught — in which universal salvation has been claimed — in which common sense and philosophy have a place, and in which the teachings of Christ are made a reality — take the trash and fiction away that clouds them all, leaving only the reality, and the all-right doctrine stands forth a bold and palpable truth.

Our life is God's life, and we *feel* it is immortal; and in this feeling we have evidence. Our life is involuntary, and so is the growth and progress of the soul. Like little children we have fancied that we make our souls grow good or bad, that we make the condition of our future destiny, that we mould and shape, and deform or symmetrize the soul while in its wayward infancy by its childish babblings and prattling in church and in society for its future existence. But where is the hand of wisdom that made us? No soul has ever fallen out of the hand of God, or ever can; no law of nature has ever ceased to act, or ever will. We are held in the arms of infinite Wisdom and infinite Power. Life's perturbations, its conflicts, and its sufferings, that come to us of what we call evil, are lawful necessities, written in the volume of nature, which volume is the statute book of the living God.

"Faith in God" is confidence in this power. "Charity" is the recognition in the goodness of God in every thing. "Have faith in God." "Perfect charity covereth a multitude of sins."

"In these views we hold the key
To faith in God and charity."

No other views of life can bring to us faith in God and charity to man.

We say that "fancy fools the world," and "evil sways humanity." Ten thousand strings make up the harp of life, and the skilful player sweeps them all in harmony, and melody is the tune of his existence; and heaven is everywhere, and everywhere is the place where God abides. The great musical instrument of God is all nature; it is in time and tune, and from it the melody of heaven shall come forth to the soul attuned thereto — "Discord is harmony," then "understood."

There is no noise in life that is not harmony to the soul that sees God in all things. The murmurings of distant waterfalls, and the murmurings and curses of humanity, are equally harmonious; the sweet songs of angels, and the groans of agony, are musical notes in harmony, that flow from the vibrations of nature's harp-strings. All the sharps and flats, the high and low sounds in the scale of human life, blend in harmony, blend in one, are inseparably connected and bound together, to make up the melody of life. God is in every note — no more in one than in another. All is beautiful, all is harmony to the soul that sees God everywhere.

The groans of agony come of suffering, which is a chariot of speed that carries the soul rapidly to the gates of happiness, and then, how beautiful shall be the fruit of what we now call a curse. The suffering that produces groans makes humanity walk in the garden of angels sooner. How wise and loving is the power that directs the soul onward and upward in its flight from darkness to light, from suffering to bliss.

I cannot doubt

> " That heaven is a place where pearly streams
> Glide over silver sands."

But it is gained by ten thousand conflicts to be first passed in the journey of life. These conflicts are the fruits of sin, and it is the decree of God that we pass through them. Every thing we call evil and sinful, is in time and place; is the necessity of the condition where they exist; created, governed, and directed by the hand of Infinite Wisdom.

Tell me where the soul can stand, except it be where it sees every thing right, and forgive seventy times seven? What is called the church of Christ forgives the murderer and the thief, not once, but by deeds of condemnation and punishment, *recriminate*, *reproduce* the crime condemned. It is impossible for a man holding these views to forgive, by actual deeds, less than seventy times seven, if needs be, no matter what the deed.

Tell me where a man can stand and resist no evil? Nowhere, except in the place where he stands when he sees no evil to resist. This doctrine sees every law of God in nature as being inevitable, unchangeable, and unalterable; a necessity in its condition—wherever it may exist—high or low—in darkness as in light—in what we call *evil*, as in what we call *good*, the same.

Judge not, says Christ. No comparison can these views level upon men by saying that one is better than another.

Lay not up for yourselves treasures on earth, but

lay up for yourselves treasures in that unseen world of spiritual existence. Take no thought for the morrow, for what ye shall eat, drink, or wear, but seek to know the hidden laws by which those things are governed, and every desire is gratified thereby. Rest in the arms of trust.

These are the precepts of Christ — enigmas to humanity, until the soul can see harmony in all things, which unriddles them, and exposes their unfading, eternal beauty to view.

OBSESSION.

There is hardly a person, who has had much experience in Spiritualism, that has not witnessed the unpleasant effects of obsessions, which, in many cases, have proved very troublesome and painful. Hundreds and thousands of mediums have, in the course of their mediumship, encountered some of the sad experiences of obsession. None are free from the liability. Those who are called the purest, the highest and the holiest, in my experience, are more the subjects of obsession than those who are called less so. The *best* mediums have been oftenest and worst obsessed. There is a great aversion, on the part of mediums and their friends, to make public any cases of this kind, because it is and has been thought that they can exist only in a low spiritual development; so that of only one case, perhaps, in a hundred that have occurred, the public have any knowledge.

In relation to obsessions, the first and most important question to be answered is: What is the cause? In the "cure" of any "evil," or any disease, the cause must be first removed. A burn cannot be cured until it is removed from the fire that produces it. Mr. Tiffany thinks that obsessions are caused by yielding control to the spirits. Here is only the effect — the thing produced. The cause lies back of this. Entrancement has fallen upon humanity without will, desire, or invitation; and innumerable well-attested instances have shown that entrancement has been produced without any knowledge of trance, or of spiritual manifestations. Little children and aged people have been seized with trance, who never sat in a circle, or had any knowledge of a spiritual manifestation; and thousands of trances have been produced, contrary to the volition of the medium, and in spite of all efforts to the contrary.

An instance of this kind took place in a Spiritualist convention in Plymouth, last year. Miss Lizzie Doten, one of the best mediums, affirmed publicly, that no spirit, even an angel from heaven, *should* control her organism independent of her *own will.* Subsequent to this, in the presence of many hundred persons, a spirit gained perfect control, and caused her to tear her collar in shreds, break her combs, and crush her bonnet into a ball not larger than a teacup. This work of the spirit proved excessively mortifying to Miss Doten, when her consciousness was restored. It was done, as the spirit declared, to show that mediums have no will independent of spirit-power. I am aware that the world might say Miss Doten deceived in this matter, and did the whole thing of her own volition. Miss Doten declares that there was no volition of her own in this act, and she is a woman of unquestioned integrity; and if there has been a life of spotless purity lived on earth, the past life of Miss Doten well merits that reputation. This instance of the superiority of spirit-power over the human will, is but one of many that has come within my limited observation.

My experience in Spiritualism forces the conclusion, daily, more and more, that mortals have intrinsically no control over spiritual influences that are ever acting upon humanity.

Can a medium allow, or not allow, herself to be controlled by spirits? She may *think* she can, as did Miss Doten. She may will, and think her will is potent, when it is only spirit-power acting in concert with her desires. The general manifestations of Spiritualism contradict the assertion that a medium's will can control spirit-power. What is, then, the cause of obsession? The hidden truths that underlie the whole subject of Spiritualism we know but little of as yet; and the great and beautiful truth that shall reveal to us the fact, that *all evil is a fruitful means of good*, though it has been hidden in darkness, now stands up for human consideration in the light of spiritual development. Self-reliance is the cause of entrancement; but self-righteousness is the cause of obsession. Both self-reliance and self-righteousness are bred in the bones of humanity, and nature alone shall carry man from the development of self-reliance and self-righteousness, to a higher development where men are conscious of the existence of, and shall rely upon an unseen Power.

What shall be done when a medium is obsessed? We say, remove the cause. How? By natural growth. Obsessions are natural; they are the legitimate effect of a natural cause; which effect becomes a new cause for the destruction of self-righteousness, of self-reliance — they bring humanity to humility — to a universal brotherhood. Greater good and greater beauty shall be developed from out obsessions, than from spiritual communications called the highest, the purest, and the holiest.

What shall we do with a case of obsession when the medium is suffering agony, and death is even threatened? We have *living hearts* to exercise, made to beat in sympathy and in love for *good spirits*, and for *evil spirits* too. Can love and sympathy fail to fill their missions? Both love and sympathy can see through the phantom of self-excellence and self-righteousness, and reach out to naked souls the offerings of affection; and the response is not antagonism, but affection. We have reason, too, to be exercised. Let us, in our feeble spiritual development, be truthful to the spirit obsessing, and not say to him, Come up from the darkness that you are in, to the light that we are in; but rather let us be conscious of our own condition, and say to the spirit, Take our hands, and lead us from the darkness that surrounds us, to the light that you possess. Let us remember that it is folly to try to cast a mote from the spirit's eye, when we have a beam in our own. Meet an obsessing spirit in the clouds of self-righteousness, and he will act very bad, and do much mischief, and befool us; meet him on the platform of common sense and reason, and he will meet us as a man. Take off the airs and phantoms of self-superiority in religion and spiritual goodness, and obsession will cease forever.

OPINIONS OF OTHERS AND REMARKS.

Letter from Justin Lillie.

"BROTHER A. B. CHILD,—Among the contributors to the *Banner of Light*, your name often appears. I read your remarks with interest, though, I must confess, some of your ideas are new to me. You say all evil is a means of the soul's development in progression. If I fathom your meaning, you claim that man is not to blame for his deeds; that he cannot help acting as he does act. I gather from what you say that man, in consequence of being low in the scale of mortality, cannot help lying or stealing, and, if in a still more degraded state, he cannot help taking the life of his brother man. Would you have it, then, that man is not accountable for his vile or sinful acts? Or would you have it that the blame lies in allowing himself to get into such a state of mind that he cannot help murder, rapine, arson, slander, hypocrisy, theft, and the like? It seems, if we place our hands in the fire, they will burn, and we shall feel the smart. If we strike the God of heaven and earth and all created things, shall we not feel pain as the result? Shall we not feel pain, also, if we strike our brother man, who is made in God's image? Shall we not feel pain if we violate any of the divine requirements?

I want you should write me, and explain particularly in regard to the foregoing."

I doubt not that the questions that have come up in your mind are the questions that a thousand have silently asked on the subject that now agitates the minds of all who love the truths of modern spiritual revelation; viz., the question of the *existence of what is called evil.*

I will answer your questions the best I can in a few words. You ask, "Is evil a means of the development of the soul?" I cannot reasonably and philosophically give but one answer to this question; viz.: What we call the evil deeds of men, are the legitimate *effects* of the soul's development; what we call the good deeds of men are the same. The soul is mightier than the effects that fall from its growth, and is, consequently, not governed by what it produces. The soul is governed by the unseen currents of God's love; is fed by streams of spirit-influx, unseen by mortal eyes, coming from a source above itself. The soul is ever living, ever active, ever growing, ever developing, under this unseen influence. In the past we have believed that what the soul produces—viz., good deeds and bad deeds—influenced its development, and in so doing we have only taken an effect for a cause. The deeds of every human soul, whether good or bad, are the effects of the development of the soul; lawfully, and perfectly in keeping with the conditions of the soul that produced them, which deeds are neither a means that can develop the soul, nor a means that can retard its development. The soul, we say, is above the material world; it is immortal; if so, it cannot be influenced by the material world; it cannot be influenced by doctrines or beliefs, by earthly teachings or earthly actions.

You say, "If I fathom your meaning, you claim that man cannot help acting as he does act, and is not to blame for his acts." I mean precisely this: no law of nature can be controverted, stayed, altered, or broken.

There is *no* human deed without a cause, and no cause that is not grasped by a law of nature.

There is a power above the human soul over which the soul has no control. That power gave it existence and continues its existence. Let that power cease to act and the soul's existence ceases. The soul did not conceive itself, or give itself birth; neither does it sustain itself or continue its existence. We must acknowledge that there is a ruling hand in human life, as there is in all life; that hand sustains, supports, directs, and guides us, and

> "In each event of life how clear
> That ruling hand we see."

Who made the soul with its conditions? and who made the laws that govern it? We acknowledge that God did these things, and that he is everywhere, and is *all-wisdom*, *all-power*, and *all-love*. If these be the attributes of God, what can exist outside of himself? Man neither creates his condition nor the laws that govern his condition. God holds every man in his own hand, more surely and lovingly than a mother holds her infant babe to her bosom. A divine hand made human conditions, and a stern demand of nature makes every man do that he does — act as he acts — and a higher, truer condition of human life will not see or attribute any blame to the so-called evil actions of men; charity accepteth all things; believeth all things. There surely is a point of progress to which the soul will attain, wherefrom it shall see no blame; it shall know no condemnation; then it shall see more of God than it now does in its earlier existence; then it will see the hand of God in hell as palpably as in heaven;

in what is called low life, as necessary as in what is called high life — in darkness as in light. The pure in heart shall see God everywhere. When we are men and women grown in spirit, we shall not condemn the infancy of our existence. The soul comes up through all the gradations of human development, from the worst evil to the highest virtue, in its progress. When it has passed the temptation of an evil, its blame and condemnation for the commission of that evil in others ceases — not before. It is then a man sees the hand of God in an evil; and it is no longer an evil in its consequences to him; for he has gained by natural growth a power over it, and his charity for those who commit it is perfect.

"You speak of lying, stealing, murdering, and other heinous crimes, and ask if man is to blame for committing them." Where shall we go for authority on this subject? Let us go to the volume of nature — the truest word of God revealed to humanity. Turn over her pages of truth, and what do we read there, in answer to this question? Where shall we find in the whole volume of this gigantic book, fresh from the hand of God, the chapter of *blame* and *responsibility?* Nowhere, nowhere! It is not there.

> "* * * Each moss,
> Each shell, each crawling insect, holds a rank
> Important in the plan of Him who framed
> This scale of being; holds a rank which, lost,
> Would break the chain, and leave behind a gap
> Which Nature's self would rue.

Is there blame because these things are lower than human intelligence? — are lower than the purity and wisdom, the beauty and love of angel life? No, there is no blame. Then, if there is no blame here, there certainly is no blame for lower grades of human intelligence, compared with higher — for lower conditions of morals, compared with higher conditions of virtues.

We turn to the page on which are written the criminal deeds of human beings, and we find there is not one deed committed without a natural cause, every deed of which cause is a natural effect; and no effect in nature is produced contrary to her laws; consequently, there is recorded no blame, no responsibility for a default in the Bible of nature, anywhere to be found.

Crime belongs to a low condition of material life, and every manifestation of crime is a lawful effect of the condition in which its causes exist. All the darker, lower steps on the ladder of human progress every soul has passed, or will pass in some manifestation of life. But in so doing, crime, with every one, may not be ultimated in physical deeds, to be tangibly perceived. Yet the power to commit these crimes that humanity is heir to, is possessed, or will be, in the lower, darker degrees of human existence, by every one.

You ask if the criminal is to blame for allowing himself to get into such a state of mind that he cannot help committing crimes? For every condition existing in human life there have been causes of sufficient power to produce them; and these causes have lain back beyond the reach of every criminal.

The light of science now enables an expert phrenologist, aided by anatomy and physiology, as he goes through the wards of a state prison, to tell to a positive certainty what the criminal deeds of each prisoner are. He can tell, too, if they are virtually innocent of the crime for which they were sentenced. He can tell unmistakably, as has been done in many cases recently, the prisoner who has committed rape, murder, theft, arson, revenge, etc. All this he tells by the temperament of the prisoner, and the formation of his brain and its developments; the brain is a natural development; it is formed by nature, and it grows by the inflowing of nature's unseen currents.

Before a child is born, it has the direction and the latent power of its destination already created; and a man will follow the bent of his natural inclinations in defiance of all the hideous phantoms that what is called religion can paint before his vision. A man is natural, and he follows nature in his spirit, in spite of all that human lips can utter; and he cannot help so doing. Man runs as naturally to do the deeds of human life that he does do, as the stream runs on its course to the place of its destination, obedient to the laws of nature. The stream may meet obstructions, and be turned a little in its onward course, and so may man, but both, governed by unalterable laws, tend onward, to their destination.

Where lies the blame in the poor criminal, for that condition of life that made him commit crime? I know no blame. God has made him what he is, and if his chains make him ache and suffer, I would to God that my sympathy was big enough to make me ache and suffer too, until his chains are broken. For the crinimal I know no demerit, and for the virtuous I know no merit. If the seeds of holiness have been planted in my soul, O God, I pray that they may bud and bloom in compassion for the criminal, and not in blame or condemnation for him.

Efforts to do good are, to me, beautiful, pleasant, and delightful, and the conflicts of sin are as painful to me, and are as unpleasant to my longings for happiness, as to you, my dear brother; but I desire to see life as it is, created and held by an unseen Hand, that worketh out good forever. I desire to speak of things as they are; to recognize the hand of God in all, not in part, of his works, and to have faith in his wisdom, power, and love; to have confidence that we are chastised for good; and without this chastisement of what we call evil, a means is wanting in the plan for the fulfilment of the great purposes of life.

Letter from S. S. W., Milton, Wis.

This letter was addressed to the *Banner of Light* and published under the head, " A. B. C."

" It is not particularly concerning the first three characters of the English alphabet that we propose to discourse, but of that which they sometimes represent.

" Some men's names are indicative of the relation they occupy to truth. There is no philosophical, metaphysical, or *spiritual* reason for this, unless we believe that a species of nomancy, or rather ariolation, has had something to do with individual destiny and the selection of cognomens; nevertheless, there often seems to be a striking coincidence between the nominal significance and the logical or ethical position of some individuals. If it were not for the many intolerable blunders she makes, one might almost believe that nature, peering into the future, adapts her handiwork to the title by which it is to be distinguished.

" But enough of this mere persiflage, since so many have had their inky fling at its subject.

" A theory is much talked of in the columns of the *Banner*, and is urged with a considerable array of analogous and, apparently, logical arguments, that evil is a normal manifestation; not, as some of this theory's opposers charge, that there is no evil, — that what we call evil is in reality good and right, but that it is one of the necessary conditions of the soul, and ultimately leads up to light and truth.

"The sum and substance of the analogy so often cited, in some one of its many forms, by the advocates of this theory, is this — that Nature, acting through the soul as she does through the physical body, ejects its bad humors — evil — as the latter does the infection of small-pox, or scarlatina, by the eruptive efforts at the surface, which we call evil, or wickedness. The analogy is drawn well enough, but not deep enough; else would the position of A. B. C. be first in the alphabet of true philosophy, as well as in that on the first page of the spelling-book; but since every manifestation of evil only tends to make its author more prone to sin, rendering him less able to resist temptation, dragging him down to a level with the crimes themselves, it follows that he who preaches 'whatever is, is right,' lacks logic in the theory, and often meets a flesh-and-blood proof of its inconsistency in practice.

"Following the same analogy, only a little deeper, there are other ways by which the physical body rids itself of morbific matter, than by 'critical determination to the surface,' as the medical savans would say. While acknowledging that this determination to the surface is a method of purification, and that it is perfectly proper to institute a comparison between the physical and the spiritual processes, it is claimed that the violent 'determination' method is not only not the best, but is among the crudest ever adopted by nature. Our common mother works faithfully and conscientiously, but she works in the dark, and her physical manifestations are not always of the highest or best character. Reason is needed to direct her action, and hence the rational endowment of man.

"Man's physical body is perhaps the most perfect type of the higher existences of which we can take cognizance through the medium of our physical senses, and whatever process of development or purification in the former is evidently the most perfect, also approximates nearest to the development process of the latter.

"Inasmuch as the most perfect method of bodily purification is not violent and eruptive, but quiet and imperceptible, it is natural to conclude that the same process in the spiritual nature is not by outbursts of grossness and wrong, but by the silent elimination of evil, and the assimilation of elevating influences — its still out-reachings after the true, the beautiful, and the good, by its energetic struggles to resist temptation, to know and do the right, and to avoid the wrong.

"If the A.-B.-C. doctrine is correct, let it be sounded forth, for truth is better than error at all times, — A. B. C. to the contrary notwithstanding,—and will eventually supersede, as we verily have faith; but if the idea that evil is one manifestation of God is lame in its logic, disastrous in its effects on the race, and tends to lower the standard of moral virtue in the world, it is time it was examined. It *is* illogical and improbable, because it robs man of all agency, and implicates the all-pure Father in the lowest and meanest manifestations of wickedness. It throws off all restraint from those who fully believe it; for who, of those inclined to sin and sensuality, would care to what depths of pollution they sank, if they felt that they were *impelled* thereto by a wise and good Creator, for some of his beneficent purposes? Even admitting that it may be true, it is evident that the world is far from being ready for it. Our private belief is, that A. B. C. is as much beyond the truth as some of his opposers are behind it; that the true position lies, as it often does, between the two extremes.

"It remains for rational minds to draw the distinction-line, each to his own satisfaction, remembering, with all diligence, that every soul must act up to its own highest conceptions of truth and right, if it would grow into the perfect stature of true manhood. S. S. W."

In answer to this very handsome letter, I cannot but express my admiration for the writer's manly treatment of the subject, though he is somewhat opposed to my views. His objections to the doctrine, "Whatever Is, is right," are the objections which I know a great many have, and for this reason I will answer those objections. My brother says:—

"Since every manifestation of evil only tends to make its author more prone to sin, rendering him less able to resist temptation, dragging him down to a level with the crimes themselves, it follows that he who preaches 'whatever is, is right,' lacks logic in his theory, and often meets a flesh-and-blood proof of its inconsistency in practice."

Such has not been my experience in life. My "evil" deeds have been as large and as numerous as the "evil" deeds of any one. I cannot deny that the ability to resist temptation after the commission of the *first* "evil" deed is lessened, and perhaps after the second, third, etc. But when I have followed and obeyed my desires in the direction of so-called evil deeds, sooner or later I have found them cloyed and satisfied, and I have turned away, and new desires have led me to seek that which we call good. The *resistance of temptation* has *never* changed my desires from "evil" to "good." Desires are natural, and will have their run; and I do not deny that the resistance of temptation is just as natural and is legitimate, in a certain condition of the soul's progress. Temptation is only a conscious desire of the soul; it is lawful and right, and the "crimes" committed in consequence are only effects of natural desires; they are the effects of the soul's life, the soul's activity; they are only the refuse matter of earthly love falling off from the soul, and by them the soul cannot be injured, any more than a tree is injured by the falling of its leaves in autumn. The tree still lives to again send off the emanations of beauty peculiar to itself; it is not dragged down to a level with its decaying foliage. The soul produces desires, and these desires produce the manifestations of life that our sensuous eyes behold in material, human existence. It is with these sensuous eyes that we see evil, wrong, conflict, and inharmony, manifested by the power of unseen life, in matter. These evils that we behold are only the natural effects of the soul, and fall from the soul like the leaves from the tree; the soul is the real life.

The "logic" of matter is a feeble thing, for to matter alone it belongs. "Flesh-and-blood proof" is no abiding evidence of soul-realities, for such proof, like flesh and blood itself, changes and falls, and again returns to the elements from which the powers of the soul have drawn it.

I do not deny that, to sensuous, limited vision, the manifestations of human life appear wrong; it is right and necessary that they should so appear. It is this natural consciousness of wrong that produces the resistance of temptation; the resistance of evil — to which condition this resistance is good and necessary, not evil or wrong. But to the vision of the soul; to its deepest conscious convictions, I boldly declare that every manifestation of human life in matter, from the bright and the beautiful to the dark and the damned, are infinitely significant of good. I do not utter this from evidence gathered from flesh and blood, nor with the perishing logic that belongs to material intelligence;

the evidence is intuition; the truth is eternal; a part of the soul's immortality.

I *would* not say that the "soul's outreaching after the true, the beautiful, and the good, and its energetic struggles to resist temptation; to know and do the right, and to avoid the wrong," and I *do* not say that this is "wrong;" I would rather say that this is *eminently right;* but I am forced to the conclusion that this is an outreaching for the glories of the material world, for the reason that the glories of the spiritual are developed, unseen, by natural growth out of the soul, fed by an unseen influx from the spiritual world, *independent of human will,* and above human control—above the influence of matter.

Some will say, in answer to this, Then you would make man an automaton? No, I would not; I would let man be just what he is. Man is just what he is, and he will be just what he will be, in defiance of all human preaching, and all efforts at human restraint. Human desires run out from a natural fountain through natural channels, to do the deeds of life, and no human effort can stay or alter them, no more than all humanity, with one combined effort, can stop the sun from shining. This mighty unseen power of the soul, that *inevitably* produces *all* the actions of men, we have yet to recognize. We yield to it in blindness, and *think that we do not.*

My brother says:—

"If the A.-B.-C. doctrine is correct, let it be sounded forth, for truth is better than error at all times." This "doctrine" *will* be sounded forth, but it will never be accepted from the tongue of material philosophy; it can be accepted only by the development of positive *intuition* in the soul that accepts it. When it is accepted, the soul will ask for no schoolhouse logic, or no material proof; this "doctrine," when developed, is developed in the soul, by its own growth, positive, abiding, and eternal. It may, then, well be asked, for what do you write? I answer, for the same material reason that others write. All writing and preaching is the effect of life, not a thing that affects the soul in any possible way.

Who will be first to accept the truth of this doctrine? It will not be the souls whose material covering wears the highest polish by earthly culture, earthly religion, and earthly training. Men of science, men of philosophy, men of religion, men of morals, men of conservative principles, and habits of rectitude and justice, men of riches, popularity, and honors, are not the men who first will seize this heavenly truth. 'Tis not the man who "knows" that he is better than another man, who is conscious of self-excellence in this world's glories, who will be willing to recognize first the great *level sea of human beings — the common level of a human brotherhood* — the one great common household of God, every child of which is equally loved, equally cared for, and has an equal claim upon the estate of his or her Father by the *will* of that same Father. Such men, I say, instead of being the first to accept the doctrine, will, for a time, be its most bitter opposers. Who, then, will first accept this doctrine? The souls whose vigorous, natural growth has burst and broken the beauty of their material existence — the downcast and the outcast, the afflicted and the chastened, the tearful and the bleeding, the naked and the hungry, the toiling slave and the bonded criminal, the despised and the rejected

—these humble flowers of God's own laws, whose love of earth is broken, *are the first.* Those who have rents and broken places in their garments of earthly love, who have naked spots upon their souls where the tendrils of angel-love can cling — such are the men and women who, by the power of intuition, shall first declare that *God is right, and all that he has made is right.* Such are those who blame not, condemn not, and whose charity accepteth all things. Such are the first who shall see God in all things. Such as these shall be the first out of whose souls the flower of intuition shall *earliest* unfold; and the truth of these words shall be proved; viz., "The last shall be first." The last in material glory shall be first in spiritual glory.

Intuition! — held for a time wisely in check by the logic and philosophy of matter, — O glorious intuition! All hail your bright and heavenly advent! The mountain of material glory is barren to the flower of intuition. Out of the valleys of the earth, rich with the corruption and decay of matter, the flower springs spontaneously, and blooms in vigorous beauty.

My brother claims that this doctrine

"*Is* illogical and improbable, because it robs man of all agency, and implicates the all-pure Father in the lowest and meanest manifestations of wickedness. It throws off all restraint from those who fully believe it; for who, of those inclined to sin and sensuality, would care to what depths of pollution they sank, if they felt that they were *impelled* thereto by a wise and good Creator, for some of his beneficent purposes? Even admitting that it may be true, it is evident that the world is far from being ready for it."

It may be illogical, and I rather think it is; for logic

is only a property of material intelligence, a property of matter; and this doctrine, in silent power, rises up to disintegrate and dissolve matter, and with it, its changeable, uncertain philosophies. Human philosophy and human logic shall be buried in the same grave with earthly affections. I do not mean to say that logic and philosophy are not true and beautiful to their place and condition; but I do say that they are things of earth, and will some time come up to maturity and fall back to dissolution. They are effects of the soul; and it is the soul only, the beautiful soul, that rises above time and the decay of matter on the wings of immortality.

This doctrine robs man of nothing; it certainly does not rob him of his free agency, or any agency, for it fully accepts human agencies as necessities of conditions out of which they spring. It accepts every exhibition of human life as being perfectly and exactly in harmony with the cause that produced the effect.

It does not implicate "the all-pure Father in meanness," for it recognizes the infinite goodness of God in *every* manifestation of his life, *in all creation.* It sees God in every thing.

In regard to this doctrine throwing off restraint for the commission of deeds of evil, I boldly declare that so long as man needs restraint, he will never accept or believe this doctrine. Restraint is necessary and lawful in its place, and so long as it is necessary and lawful, so long will it exist. This doctrine accepts the legality of restraint no less than the legality of crime. Both are necessary, or else why did the infinite power of God show them to us?

That this doctrine throws off restraint, and gives unbridled license to crime, is a favorite and almost universal argument that a love of *materialism* brings against it. A man that needs the bridle of restraint, when he reads this doctrine, rises up with a burst of rage, and says, "Good God! what an awful, damnable doctrine is this! Why, if I believed it, I would plunge headlong into all the crimes of licentiousness; I would steal, lie, rob, murder, fight, and do every thing that I have a desire to do. Why, the man who utters such awful doctrine, should be branded with infamy, and the papers that publish such doctrine should be blotted out of existence!"

This man needs restraint a little longer, and he will certainly have it; the laws that govern his nature demand it. His fear demands the resistance of evil, and resistance is right to his condition. This man is good, but he is youthful in his spiritual development.

But let us go a little further. Suppose that this man was inclined to sensuality, and in consequence of this doctrine, did not, at first care to what depths he sank in pollution. Let him obey his desires, and go on in such a course to his heart's content. How long, think you, before the fires of hell would drive him back? How long, think you, before the filth and fetor of such a life would satiate his desires, and nauseate his material life with disgust? As it was with the prodigal son, so it would be with him. The prodigal's course was restrained by the laws of nature.

Human desires will always find vent, sometime or somewhere, sooner or later, in darkness or in light, whether in keeping with human law, or against it, always in obedience to natural law — in spite of all *pretence*.

All the manifestations that we call evil, have their payment "*down*," in pain and suffering, and it is nature that deals the "wages" out; and it is in wisdom and in justice that she measures the suffering for each. The measure is never too large or too small, but exactly meets the demand. A true hand, and a nicely balanced hand, too, is this hand of nature. A wise and beneficent hand, also, is this hand of nature. With infinite skill her fingers work out all the deeds of human life and all life.

No human being loves suffering. No human being asks for or desires pain. You tell a man that suffering is soul-progression, and let him believe what you tell him, and also possess an ardent longing for progress, even then he will not voluntarily suffer. Nobody voluntarily plunges into pain. Human volition is against human suffering. The cup of bitterness humanity drinks from, but never by choice; not even did Christ do this. It is in the ordering of nature that we *must* suffer; it is the will of God, and "thy will, O God, not mine, be done." I know all is for good.

Disease, accidents, earthly rents, breaks, and tears; revenge, hate, cruelty, and oppression; poverty, ignorance and crime, with their endless retinue of miseries, are the antagonizing and necessary elements which *material reason* meets. It is this conflict that keeps the works of nature balanced up; that stirs the sands of earth around the tender germs of eternal life that are planted in earth to bloom in heaven — the beautiful souls of women and men.

Suffering, by human volition, it is neither enhanced nor retarded. It *will* come in one way or another by the hand of God himself in nature. And what we call evil deeds are always rewarded by suffering. These "evil" deeds are involuntary; they come from natural desires. A deep examination of human life will prove this statement true. I think that evil deeds, so called, are the effect of an early expansion of the soul in matter, that break earthly beauty, and free the soul sooner. This can *never* be *voluntary*, for pain and suffering our volition turns from ever. We cannot do more of evil than our inclinations lead us to; and we cannot do more of good than our inclinations lead us to do. There is an almighty power behind the curtain of material vision that moves humanity to do the deeds of life that humanity does do.

And the day has come when this power begins to be recognized — this power of *spirit-reality*. And in the recognition of this power, all *doctrines* and *beliefs*, all writing and preaching, lecturing and loud praying, will come up to the "valley of decision," where all things of earth must come *for judgment*, and fall back to decay as being no longer useful to the soul that has cast them off.

Do not fear, my brother, the influence of this or any other doctrine, for doctrines are only effects of the soul — are things of time — not properties of the soul's eternal life.

Extract of Letter from Y. C. Blakey, M.D.

"My brother, when I commenced reading your articles on the subject of 'Whatever Is, is Right,' your boldness at first startled me; but the more I read and reflect on them, the more I find my judgment acquiescing in the position you have taken."

I feel a sure confidence that all who are at first startled with the "all-right" doctrine will, on further reflection, aided by an accompanying development of intuition find their judgment acquiescing in the beautiful truth.

Extract of a Letter from E. Annie Kingsbury.

"The philosophy, of 'Whatever Is, is Right,' inculcated by you through the columns of the *Banner of Light* is to me very beautiful; it is substantial, satisfying, and divine. It is an elucidation of ideas which for four years I have boldly spoken to my friends in private, and you may be sure it now delights me to see them so ably presented and so widely circulated. This philosophy has done me much good; it has sustained me in the midst of trials, terrible and protracted, and it will assuredly benefit every one who studies and appropriates it. In the name of humanity, let me thank you for the good you are doing. You are blessed already with the possession of a peace and harmony of spirit to which many others are a stranger. Permit me to say, also, that I have conversed with others in this city (Philadelphia), who rejoice in the truths you advocate."

Many beautiful souls like that of the above writer, here and there, all over the land, have already intuitive unfoldings that have aided, unseen, in the development of this doctrine A much larger number, I doubt not, than any one has thought.

Extract of a Letter from "Maggie."

"If all that is, is right, what objects have we to seek in life? why should we endeavor to remove obstacles that lie in the way of the soul's progress?"

The writer of this question does not recognize the fact that our endeavor to remove obstacles that lie in the way of the soul's progress is a part of what is right in our existence, just as much as the obstacles that are thought to lie in the way of the soul's progress are incident to our existence. Both the obstacles that lie in our way, and the efforts to remove them out of our way, must be right, if both exist. The writer continues: —

"When we see an individual surrounded by bad influences, degraded and suffering, in whom exists the elements of a noble nature — if we are conscious that all is right, we must say that his condition is right too, and let him grovel on, and sink deeper in degradation. Then what is fraternal love worth, if we cannot benefit our suffering brother?"

Seeing that every thing is meant to be as it is by an overruling Wisdom, does not stand between relief, between the manifestations of fraternal love, and human suffering, and human degradation; this doctrine does not claim that it is wrong to mitigate pain, or that it is wrong that there should be pain to mitigate. There is no manifestation of our earthly life more beautiful than efforts to relieve human woe. We know that woe exists, and for it there must be a cause, and when we see that cause, we shall see that in the end it is for good, that its existence, and its means of relief, are always twin-born; *both* are *lawful* in creation, *both* are *right*. So our efforts to relieve suffering are not lessened by a conscious conviction that suffering is meant for good. Again, Maggie continues: —

"If Dr. Child's cold doctrine of "*all* right" is true, what becomes of the beautiful theory, that the very joys of the angels consist in elevating unto them selves those who are on a lower plane of being?"

What is the work of life but a rising upward forever of the soul? and for every step in the soul's progress there is existing a cause, there must be an agency. This doctrine of *all right* is not opposed to the holy, unselfish work of angels, which is to this end — which is the immediate agency in the work of human elevation. The soul that can see angels doing this holy work, can also see the lawful cause of degradation that commands this work — can see every thing in the chain of cause and effect, from angel life to the lowest (if low in spirit there be) plane of human existence as being in time, in perfect tune — as being in perfect harmony in the reality of the spirit, and palpably see that all apparent discord in the physical world is perfect harmony in the spiritual world, which spiritual world pervades and produces the material world.

This doctrine of "all right" does not dim the reality of angel existence, nor influence their holy mission to bring us to heaven. It magnifies both in the real conceptions of our souls. It may be that angels in wisdom deal out suffering to us, and then sustain us while we endure it, for our advancement.

A writer in the *Spirit Guardian* asks the following question: —

"If there is no evil, Bro. Child, it is, of course, not right that man should be punished for any of his deeds, be they ever so bad; he may murder his fellow-man, and still be allowed to go at large; to take the life of others and inflict a thousand wrongs upon his fellow-creatures. What shall be done with him? Shall we try to make him better?"

I cannot claim that it is wrong for a man to be punished for crime, for the reason that no deed is wrong.

The criminal is punished, and suffers. I know no reason why this is not right; and I know no reason why the crime is wrong. Both crime and punishment are links in the chain of cause and effect, in the courses of nature; they are legitimate to that condition of life that produces them.

Every thing in creation is from the hand of the Creator. If man takes his brother's life, there is a cause in creation that makes him take it. If one nation slay another, there is a cause in creation that produces the slaughter. There is no law broken thereby; but the law of God in nature is fulfilled by the acting cause in spirit, that lies behind the deeds.

The deeper we look into the causes of human actions, the nearer we come to the conclusion that there is no distinction of merit and demerit to be instituted between the *good man* and the *bad man*, for the same stern and unalterable causes of nature impel both to action; the same God of wisdom has created both, and holds both in his protecting hand of love.

Prison-houses, court-houses, meeting-houses, school-houses, and state-houses, with their uses and purposes, are the lawful products of the spirit of man in a certain condition of development; and in the present condition of society they are necessary and right.

One writer says:—

"Dr. Child has an angle—a hobby which he rides into every thing. Dr. Child says that there is no difference in things in this world."

Nature, to me, has infinite variation. Things vary in form, in size, in density, in quality, in strength, in durability; and this difference in things, which is even palpable to the dreams of a sleeping man, makes variations in the things of creation which fill up life with unutterable beauty.

If my brother means that I have an angle and a hobby which runs out to level the fiction of human distinctions; to take the starch out of self-righteousness; to show how nonsensical and unmeaning, as applied to human souls, the words *high* and *low*, *evil* and *good* are, it seems to me he might indulge a sinner like me in running an angle, and riding a hobby, that differs somewhat from an angle and hobby of self-righteousness, of hell and damnation that has been ridden into every meeting-house pulpit, and into every school-house desk of education in the civilized world, and from thence has been driven into the hearts of the good people, from a period of time to which my memory goeth not back. The hobby that makes one man better than another, in a spiritual sense, has been ridden a great while by us all. Change is not *detrimental* to human progress, but is essentially an element of progression.

Suppose that we get off from the old hobby of evil, that runs all its riders into the contentions of hell, to fight with angles as acute as the points of bayonets and pitchforks, and mount the hobby of "Whatever Is, is right," what is the consequence? With the fleetness of thought and the surety of eternal truth, this hobby — if you please to call it a hobby — will bear us through all the beautiful gardens; through all the avenues of truth in God's creation; and everywhere at out pleasure we may pick flowers of unfading freshness from the provinces of God, in the eternal day-time of his love, forever.

This is the hobby, and this alone, that shall carry humanity out from the darkness and sufferings of hell. Each one must mount it and ride it for himself and herself.

This little "hobby" horse of "*all-right*," we at first think is wanton, shy, coltish, *dangerous*. That day is coming when every man and every woman will in one voice declare, that this hobby is the gentlest and the kindest, the safest and the truest, the fleetest and the boldest "hobby" ever rode upon. But no man or woman will ever be lifted upon it by another; will ever mount it till he or she does it voluntarily; till by natural growth the soul is rid of the shackles of fear and the darkness of self-righteousness; till the heart is purified from the love of matter sufficiently to see God in every thing.

Letter from A. P. Mc Combs.

"That there is a vast amount of evil in the world, and that the proofs of its existence are everywhere self-evident, is the almost universal belief of mankind. 'Tis true, there are a limited number of persons who hold an adverse theory, and the writer concurs in the sentiment, 'Nature has done all things well;' and that all animated beings, and inanimate creation, are subject to, and controlled by, natural laws, and, indeed, form a part of nature herself; and, of course, it would be presumptuous folly to suppose that nature could violate her own laws. Consequently, we contend that no absolute evil ever did take place in the whole history of the world.

"God, as the Creator and Progenitor of the universe, infused and breathed life and motion into all things, from his own person, and has left the impress of his hand and mind on all his works, and so they all reflect their Author. And in no particular does the infinite wisdom of the Creator more strikingly shine forth, than in the great variety with which he has stamped every department of nature.

"Narrow and unthinking minds will pronounce these views as the veriest nonsense and wildest folly; and it is only the unprejudiced, philosophical, and comprehensive mind, that can fathom the subject in all its various bearings, and trace the beauty, harmony, and beneficence that pervade all nature, and reign throughout the entire universe.

"Now we behold that man — related as he is, socially and fraternally, to his fellow-man and to all nature around him — is just precisely such a creature as he ought to be, physically, mentally, and morally; and that without his inclinations, tastes, dispositions, feelings, wants, desires, and passions, he would be imperfect.

"We hear it asserted, in tones of despondency, that here we are subject to pain and toil; that here we must know sorrow and become acquainted with grief, doomed to disease and death; and we assert, that where there is no pain or toil, there is, of necessity, no pleasure or rest; and if there were no sorrow or grief, the exhilarating influence of joy and gladness would never be felt; and without disease and death, there would be no health or life. If our physical nature did not require nourishment and food, and make its wants known, we could not partake and enjoy the luxuries which nature furnishes to supply those wants with that sweet relish we do. If we were not susceptible to fatigue and weariness, how could we enjoy the refreshing influences of slumber and rest? And so it is with every feeling and faculty of man; were it not so, we should be mere passive, stationary, lifeless substances.

"For the purpose of illustrating our position more fully, we will take up the traits in the human character that are almost universally condemned.

"Selfishness is everywhere denounced; but all will admit that we ought to possess the principle to a limited extent, in order to the protection, preservation, and comfort of ourselves and those dependent upon us; and who is competent to mark the precise point to which our selfishness shall extend? We say no one, because the judgments of men disagree; and ever-varying circumstances will render any fixed rule of action impracticable. Hence let this emotion in man's nature be governed by opposing traits in his own character, or the sentiments of his fellows, and the laws of the land in which he lives. So it is with hatred. No sane man would desire its entire eradication from the human breast. Hatred and discontent are great auxiliaries to the advancement of the world. We hate and dislike men, customs, and deeds that are not compatible with our notions of right, and our influence controls and changes them to a certain degree. Discontent is simply a desire to acquire more knowledge or happiness than we already possess, and has been prominently exhibited in all the great men that have left their mark in the world.

"Revenge is a heaven-born principle that God has ingrafted in every living thing beneath the sun; and all, from the huge mastodon of the forest and the mighty leviathan of the watery deep, to the smallest microscopic animalcule that floats through the air or sea, have their means and weapons of aggression and defence, and wise nature teaches them when, where, and how to make use of them for their own safety and defence.

"Revenge also holds up to the view of mankind the punishment that vicious acts merit and receive, and thereby checks, restrains, and prevents their too oft recurrence.

"But, to sum up all, murder, according to general belief, is the highest grade of crime. Spiritualism has demonstrated the fact that man lives after he leaves the body. The destruction or decomposition of the body, and, in fact, all material substances, is necessary for the recuperation of nature, to enable her to reproduce. The existence of one part of creation depends upon the destruction of another. The life of one is brought forth and nourished by another's death. 'Big fish live on little fish.' Nature accommodates herself to all her wants. It is necessary for man's own existence and happiness that he should die. Man's life in the body is terminated variously, and we hold that he cannot die an unnatural death. Sometimes by pain and sickness, cold and heat, famine and gluttony, earthquakes and storms, wars and pestilence, and sometimes by the hand of the assassin. We challenge the world to prove that the ultimate good and happiness of a single individual has ever been blasted by any of these agencies that have deprived any of the human family of their earthly existence. We believe it is for their present and future good. This is especially apparent to believers in the doctrine of departed friends returning as guardian spirits to watch over those left behind.

"I will endeavor to answer the most prominent queries and objections usually put forth by believers in man's natural depravity, against the positions here assumed, as briefly and pointedly as I can. I am asked if I advocate and believe murder is right? and, if it is no crime, is it not wrong to punish the murderer, and folly to preach reformation to man, or endeavor to correct his ways? If the assassin is only acting in conformity with the laws of nature, which you say are right, how is it that guilt and fear take possession of him, and remorse causes him to fancy that his forehead is stained with blood, and finally drives him to insanity or suicide? If your doctrines were promulgated and universally embraced by mankind in their present state, would not every law, both human and divine, be disregarded and trampled upon, and violence and crime, in all their most hideous forms, stalk forth unchecked, with a satanic smile of triumph upon their brutal lips, and run riot, until all would become maddened and frenzied with blood; and every species of crime, at which the heart of humanity sickens and fears to contemplate, be perpetrated, and devastation and ruin overspread our happy land; and from every corner of the globe, where now reigns comparative peace and order, be heard the wailings of unutterable woe?

"I answer, I do not advocate murder, neither do I believe it a positive evil; I judge the punishment or penalty affixed thereto. By the same law, it would be irrational to make an exception in favor of the criminal. Nature regulates her government by wise provisions; one act follows another in natural order. I believe it right and proper to preach and teach what we believe, and endeavor to reform our race, for the very reason that nature makes use of these means to accomplish her purposes, and her own advancement; therefore, I do not consider that a Christ, a Mahomet, a Napoleon, a Wesley, a Washington, or a Beecher, are exceptions in nature, or that they have lived in vain. Man, by nature, through education, the laws and opinions of the people among whom he lives, forms opinions in his own mind of right. If he acts contrary to those convictions, nature, true to herself, will punish the actor, for his own benefit, as well as to deter him and others from going further than she wills.

"Before answering the last query, permit me to digress a moment, in order that my ideas may be more fully understood. The varied and transitory character of nature is everywhere conspicuous; she has adorned the earth with every conceivable color, and everywhere we behold her surpassing beauties. We behold the lofty mountains and broad valleys, the mighty forests and barren deserts, the bubbling fount and mighty ocean, the calm and the storm, summer's heat and winter's cold, sunshine and rain, night and day. And as the phrenologist decides in regard to a nicely balanced head, that the development of one organ rules another, we contend all heads are rightly balanced; and individuals, and even nations, may be considered as bumps on creation's cranium, where the fingers of the Deity move with unerring wisdom. The universe is a vast machine, guided by a master-hand; and mankind, like unskilled mechanics looking at a complicated and perfect piece of machinery, are not able, at present, to comprehend the whole, or know the design of all its workings or its parts.

"All men are similar in their construction; yet, among the many millions that inhabit the globe, no two can be found so much alike that they could not be distinguished. We will have the active mind of the reader to determine the disastrous results that would inevitably ensue, in all the relations of life, if man's identity were lost. Therefore, if man's varied physical construction is necessary to his own well-being, it is equally so in regard to his moral, intellectual, and spiritual composition; hence every diversity of opinion prevails among mankind. We do not think, feel, believe, and act alike; and, indeed, there is not to be found among the whole human race two persons whose opinions are precisely alike on all subjects; therefore we rationally conclude that the principles we here inculcate will not be universally adopted. Centuries may elapse before the world will be far enough advanced to receive them; but when — if ever — it does, the most happy results must certainly follow.

" But I might give a more practical answer, by saying that all the vicious, degraded, and criminal of our country, disbelieve the principles here laid down, while those believing them (as far as my knowledge extends) are persons whose characters ought to be held up by all Christendom, as patterns worthy of imitation by all lovers of virtue, good order, and peace. It is therefore apparent that the prevalence of these sentiments would banish from the earth ignorance, and intolerance, its handmaid, which is certainly an end to be devoutly wished for."

The following is from the pen of my good brother, Warren Chase:—

"I rejoice to see so much written on this subject, good and evil, and to hear so much said. Agitation of thought, scepticism, and criticism are signs and beginnings of knowledge and wisdom — *not* the fear of the Lord, as has often been said. When I see an article on good and evil, or either of them, I first look at the name of the author, to see whose spectacles I am to read through. * * * * * *

"Not only do nations have different standards of good and evil, and all religious, moral, social, and political societies, but individuals in the same society often differ as widely as societies. What is good and what is evil, are questions which no God's Word Revelation, or scientific demonstration, has ever answered; therefore every speculating and theorizing mind answers for itself, or for as many others as will accept the answer, instead of thinking out answers for themselves.

"This is the basis of such societies as have organizations to carry out what they call good, and to resist what they call evil. * * * * *

"Thus I judge of good and evil, but only for myself. I will not condemn my neighbor; I am not *his* judge, but I *am my own*."

A western correspondent says:—

"I think Dr. Child is in an error when he says all writing and preaching are the effects of life, not things that affect the soul in any possible way. This I cannot comprehend."

That there is a cause for writing and preaching, no one will deny. This cause exists in the soul of man, and produces writing and preaching. So writing and preaching are the effects of the soul — are the effects of life. My convictions have forced me to take the hitherto untrodden ground, viz., *That what the soul produces cannot in any possible way influence it, either to advance or retard its progress.* All the manifestations of human life that we see with our earthly vision, are effects of human souls — are the products of causes which we cannot see except with the sight of intuition. We have judged of the soul by the standard of its effects, which effects are changeable, uncertain, unenduring, and capricious. From these effects we can know but little, if any thing, of the soul's reality. Our knowledge of the soul has been based on a standard of material things, and, like material things, is changeable and perishing. Intuition goes deeper and reaches causes that produce those physical effects; and in these causes exists reality that is enduring, abiding, and eternal.

All writing and preaching, like all the deeds of human life, both good and bad, are effects of the life of the ever-growing, ever-progressing, beautiful, immortal soul; all of which, I boldly affirm, do not and cannot have any influence to injure or benefit this indestructible reality — the soul of man. The soul possesses the elements of eternal life; so, we say, it possesses the elements of eternal progression; then it must possess the latent germ that shall forever continue to be developed to produce its progression. Truth grows out of the soul by the expansion of the latent germ that constitute its immortality. A truth was never driven into the soul of one man by another man, from the external world, that ever became a property of its immortality. The first truth and every truth that becomes a reality to the soul's eternal existence must of necessity be of intuition.

The writer continues :—

"Again, I cannot see how 'the soul's out-reaching after the true, the beautiful, and the good, is an out-reaching for the glories of the material world!'"

What we have called the good, the true, and the beautiful, are things of our existence, that so appear to our physical senses, to our conscious, tangible existence. I cannot but recognize virtue as being the crowning glory of the material world, which is an effect of the spirit; a property of earth, not of the spiritual world. All recognized religions are of the glories of the material world. Morality, equity, and justice, are of the glories of the material, not of the spiritual, world. All the deeds of kindness and love, all efforts in goodness, are effects of the soul, and are of the glories of the material world. These things in part constitute what we call the true, the beautiful, the good. These are some of the glories and the beauties of the material world; some of the effects of the soul made manifest through matter. But let the curtain of material love be drawn aside, and the vision of the soul behold its own realities, and all the glories of the earth disappear in the greater beauty of its higher and more real glories. The writer again continues: —

"I cannot see how those whose actions are the worst, develop in soul the most rapidly."

I do not mean to be understood that it is bad actions that develop the soul rapidly, but rather that bad actions are the effect of rapid soul-development. It is the soul's development that moves us to do bad deeds — deeds that result in a deformity of our material excellence, which deformity breaks our material glory, and kills our earthly love. This development of soul we have no control over. Bad actions destroy all the love of "the true, the beautiful, and the good" of the earth, and also produce pain, and render our earthly existence less attractive, and the soul is sooner freed of earthly ties, for its exit to the spiritual world, where the tendrils of its affection will cling with a power equal to its growth.

I do not mean to say that it is not commendable and right to love and cherish the true, the beautiful, and the good, in our material existence; but I do say we shall do this just in proportion as we are impelled to do it, by an overruling Power that deals with us in wisdom.

Letter from a Correspondent of the "Banner of Light."

"I have lately seen several articles published in your very interesting paper, upon the *one idea*—'Whatever Is, is Right'—and desiring to learn the truth, have thought much about it, but cannot subscribe to the doctrine that 'Whatever Is, is' *always* 'right,' and consider the teachings dangerous, as respects *time*, although they may not be so as regards *eternity*.

"Let us analyze the saying, and see how it will stand the test. Whatever is, or is transpiring, I take for granted is past, no matter how brief the period of its taking place. If what is past is *always* right, there could be no penalty attached to any act, however heinous, nor a reward bestowed for actions which are good. Spirit revelations prove that those who have left the form, suffer for wrongs done in the body. If whatever is, is right, wherefore do they suffer?

"Further: wrong committed may leave a sting, both to the perpetrator and the injured, and time, or a part of eternity (so long as spirit and matter are combined), must bear the consequences, or balance the account. If this were not so, conscience would be a blank, and virtue a chimera.

"Wrong is evil done, and must remain so, until it is overcome with good, or is righted — and cannot be called right until it is made so. One man may wrong his brother in a thousand ways, or he may be a thief, a liar, or a murderer; but can all these deeds be counted right because eternity eventually will neutralize them? No one doubts that eternity will do; but until wrong is righted, whatever is, cannot be *always* right as respects time, but may be as regards eternity.

"So long as spirit is combined or linked with matter, it will be clogged and subject to the laws of matter, and the combination or juxtaposition, in the various faculties of the brain, produce all the varieties of mind, and consequent actions for good or evil, as the one or the other predominates, is exercised or not, or influenced or not, by circumstances, the will, or the judgment. Phrenologists, it is true, are enabled, as they pass through the wards of a state prison, to tell, almost to a positive certainty, what the criminal deeds of each prisoner may have been; but they also know that if these same criminals should reform, in the course of a few years, the brain, or certain organs of the brain, will change also, so that the effects will be visible externally, not only in the physiognomy of the individual, but the various parts of the skull will be elevated and depressed, as the organs have been respectively active or dormant. This fact cannot be controverted, and puts to flight all notions that man cannot be influenced by circumstances or education.

"All children are not born with the same amount of brain, or with faculties which are alike in size, temperament, or quality; but this does not prove that these faculties cannot be cultivated, or, by exercise and proper direction, be increased in bulk, power, and quality, like the muscles of the arm, or any other part of the body. No one doubts that man has natural inclinations, but must he follow them? Cannot circumstances control the mind as well as shackles the body? Circumstances may make, even those who are better disposed, criminals. God has made all, but circumstances are permitted, and may even turn a river from its legitimate channel.

"Charity attaches no blame; but so long as the spirit is connected with matter, good (being positive in its nature) must work out, or neutralize the evil committed. Every cause must have its effect, and the further you recede from good, the greater the consequent evil. Call things by what name you please, the further you depart from the one principle, the nearer you approach the opposite.

"All existing principles are antagonistic, opposite: or, if you please, positive and negative, or, in the sexes, masculine and feminine.

"God the great I Am,—the Soul-Principle,—Creator and ever-creating Entity, is love—pure, harmonious, and homogeneous love, and is the only individual, single, self-positive, or masculine existing principle.

"All other created things, from light to the most ponderable substances in nature or the universe, are matter, and *compound* in their natures, and negative or feminine in their relation to the all Soul-Principle, or to God, the great I Am. Love, the Soul-Principle, or the spirit essence, is antagonistic to, or the opposite of, matter, or love to hatred,—good to evil,—right to wrong,—truth to falsehood, or wisdom to ignorance, etc., etc. In the sexes,—male and female,—in inanimate nature,—light and darkness, heat and cold, positive and negative electricity, magnetism and galvanism, motion and *vis inertia*, attraction and repulsion, and all the other forces in nature,—are qualities possessed by and inherent in matter, and, like all other things, are opposites, and must be neutralized before harmony, order, and perfect goodness can be attained in any case. Therefore, whatever is, may be wrong in *time*, but must be right in *eternity*."

On reading the above the following is suggested. Whatever is, is right, may be a "one idea," but it is an idea that is not developed in the soul until the soul is at peace and in harmony with all other ideas.

Time is a fractional part of eternity; the eternal years of our existence have already begun. Truth is never dangerous, whether it be developed in the soul in time, or after time. Truth, when developed by the soul, becomes a property of the soul's eternal existence.

Penalties attached to past actions, and rewards bestowed for good actions, must be right, if all things are right, and have been. The all-right doctrine does not go against penalties for crime, nor rewards for goodness. It goes against *nothing* that exists; it is at peace with all human actions, and in harmony with all life. Herein lies the great feature of beauty in this doctrine; all fault-finding and condemnation, inharmony, war, and opposition, with a conscious development of this truth, ceases to exist in the soul forever, and the millennium of peace triumphs over the inharmony that has been necessary in the past.

I do not doubt that millions "who have left the physical form suffer for deeds done in the body." This fact does not weigh against the all-right doctrine. The change we call death, does not change the development of the soul. The soul may wear for a time its garments of earthly love after, the same as before, death. All deeds are necessary products of the soul's development, and many deeds inevitably produce suffering. When the soul grows, it always produces some deeds of which suffering is the consequence; and it is this suffering that breaks the soul's affection for earth and lets it go up to light and freedom, where its nature draws it. Suffering may be as necessary after as before death. The spirit may have earthly love after, as well as before, death, and in its progress, this love will sometime be cut asunder; and suffering is the means, in the hand of Infinite Wisdom, that does this work. It is right, it is beautiful, for it frees the soul from darkness and conflict, to soar away to the condition of its deepest longings—peace, harmony, light.

"Conscience" to the soul *is* a "blank," and virtue to the soul *is* a "chimera." To the excellence of the material world conscience *is* a beautiful reality, and virtue is *not* a chimera. Conscience and virtue are attributes of the material world, and in the highest sense are beautiful in the logic of matter. In the beauty of the soul's superior attributes, when developed, conscience and virtue fade away, and, like other things of earth, cease to be.

What we call wrong is a necessary shadow of earthly love; when the love of spirit comes, this shadow is gone; the shadow needs no righting, for wrong does not then exist.

Spirit is never governed by human laws, or by the laws of matter. Matter is produced by spirit; the laws that govern the material world are produced by spirit; and, being the product of spirit, under the government of spirit, do not in any possible way affect the spirit at all. In our early and feeble soul-growth, and in our yet necessarily darkened condition, we conclude, and positively affirm, that our earthly efforts reach the soul and influence it in its development; that by physical training, moral culture, and intellectual efforts, the immortal soul is turned, is changed, in the course of its eternal destiny. This conclusion and affirmation is not a fact to the sight of intuition, but it may be a fact to the dark philosophy of matter. Man may be influenced by circumstances and education in his material being, but his soul cannot.

"Man has natural inclinations, but must he follow them?" He will always in spirit follow and obey them, and, so far as he can, he will in the material, outer world.

The circumstances of earthly things may turn a river from its legitimate channel, it is true; but they will never turn the rivers of God's eternal spirit that flow into the channels of immortal souls.

There exists in matter principles, antagonisms, and opposition — not in spirit. Principles, rules, antagonisms, and oppositions, are but playthings of the spirit's infancy; not useful in spirit-manhood. Hatred, falsehood, ignorance, darkness, are only curtains let down to keep the too dazzling light of heaven off the infant soul at first.

The following letter is from the able pen of Miss Emma Hardinge, written by request, expressly for a place in the pages of this book; and it may not be out of place to say here, that I know no *earthly angel* whose unmitigated efforts are more unselfishly devoted to relieve the sufferings of the down-trodden, the offcast, and the bleeding children of earth, than are those of Miss Emma Hardinge: —

Emma Hardinge's Letter.

"I read it in the dim twilight — in the gray hour when God's works and man's works look fitfully through the vale of gathering shadows in strange and unreal shapes. Forms most beautiful in the clear sunlight loom up mysteriously through the dimness, like grotesque phantoms and hideous distortions. The light, the truth, are wanting, and the straining vision translates beauty, through its own ignorance, into ugliness, God's goodness into wrath, and things of loveliest perfection into terror and imperfection. Is not this life? I asked. This landscape, so glorious to-day, in the broad revelation of meridian light, remains unchanged; but the medium of my vision, now obscure, transmutes the beauty into strange, mysterious pictures of black phantoms, that, now outstretched before me, show like God's great universe beheld through the mists of ignorance, and the twilight hue of prejudice. Yon lovely willow, upon whose tender green I gazed to-day with such heartful admiration, whose sheltering tresses protected me like a mother's flowing locks, looks now, in the thickening gloom, while its arms are tossed hither and thither by the wild, sad evening breeze, like a wailing widow, casting her dishevelled hair abroad in frantic grief, while her stately neighbor, the noble pine, seems pointing with spectral fingers to the very skies, in whose clear sunlight it showed to-day, a thing of proudest glory and rejoicing. Ignorance is sorrow, fear, and doubt — *not bliss.* Wisdom alone is God-revealed, and in that revelation lies full trust and satisfaction, confidence and joy. 'Look through the gloom,' my guardian spirit whispered; 'and though the light is mercifully tempered to suit thine own dim vision, 'tis full enough to read "a fragment from a page of gold."

"'I saw a band of men, all travel-stained and weary. They had walked so long and far their feet were bruised and bare, their garments worn and ragged; their sinking limbs almost refused to bear them, yet on they struggled still. I saw in their haggard faces the lines of desperate purpose — pale, pinching penury, yet savage greed of gold. Hungry they were for bread, yet hungrier still for gain. March on, march on! through flood and fell, through moss and brier, through wind and storm, in hardship, peril, heat, and cold! What earthly pain can stay them? for are they not the seekers for an empire, the pilgrims of a SUN — the only sun they wish to shine upon them — the sun of wealth? Gold-diggers, on! The goal is reached. I see them toil as never human toiled, and know, unless a magnet mighty as this gold attracted them, the mortal frame would never rend itself in labor so appalling. They have found it now — and what a thing they've found! — a rude, misshapen lump, half soil, half stone, with here and there a speck of dull, pale metal. Is this indeed the end? These wasted lives, these bleeding feet, these months of toil and effort! Some of the band are dead — perished upon the very heaps they have dug for; the ugly mounds, of mixed, coarse stuff they have lost their lives to find, their cold death pillow; — the black hard earth from which they have torn their treasure, their winding-sheet.

"'No matter; follow the gold; this is our final aim. Again, with uncounted leagues of rugged country, with months of painful toil, and jealous watching, some worn-out pilgrims reach the distant scene, where another chapter opens for the gold's progression. I see the mighty hammers crushing out its atoms; vast machines are there, invented long ago; the iron which for ages lay hidden within the mountain—the iron which for ages man has worked upon, heated and cooled, beat and drowned and burned, until, in many untold generations, he learned to fashion it so that now, attached to sides of oak and elm (grown in the ancient hours of youngest time, and hardened in the womb of ages, also), this iron, with its aides-de-camp of fire and air and water, its wheels and cranks and levers, cylinders and bands, can crush and tear the shapeless lumps, for which the miners died, into dust and powder. I see it lie in heaps; 'tis still unlovely, a sordid yellow dust — no use nor beauty. Oh, to give life for this!

"'I see great fires — the product of vast mines — of ancient forests hardened into coal; the work of flooding torrents, the crystalizing labor of old time; and lastly, the hard-won blocks torn up by thousand miners. Millions of years God labored to make these blocks; millions of men have perished to procure them; and now they blaze in the vast chimerian caverns, spending their burning rage upon the caldrons where the dull gold lies melting and fusing. Days and weeks and months great buildings are raised to shelter it, engines to work it, fires to burn, water to cool, and thousands of hands to tend it. The mighty brains that fashioned these devices! The neat, ingenious fittings of each part! How every screw and joint and lever was all invented in some busy brain, that spun, and cracked at last, thus to adjust them; — and all for what? Why, just to convert the rock's rough heaps from lumps to atoms, atoms into dust, dust into liquid, liquid into bars; bars of one shape into bars of another; and in all shapes or any, what less lovely than these dull, senseless, yellow lumps of earth? And still they burn and cool and batter on; and days and months and twelvemonths — on they go, from spot to spot, from continent to island, and still in every shape and every form, a brighter lustre looms up from out the hammer's blow, and burning caldron's glow.

"'I look at last with pleasure upon that shining face, where something of the sunlight seems to peep out reflected; and now the last blow is struck and cut within the arms of mighty-tempered steel machines, a perfect circle shines, and now one more hard grip; the crushing weight descends; a regal picture leaves its impress there, and lo! the golden guinea stands complete, the empress of the world! the sovereign's strength! the legislator's aim! the stateman's goal! the merchant's fondest hope! the beauty's conqueror! the artist's prize! the king of earthly kings! lord of the human race!

"'I could no further trace that guinea's destiny, unless I might with far out-reaching eye compass the breadth of earth. One only chapter could I read; it was within the circle of the gold whereon was stamped the image of a man. I saw him prophesied when first the ancient monsters lorded it on earth. Destructive and acquisitive they were, like the gold-diggers; their own fierce natures preying on each other, filled up the rocks with bones, swept off the excess, and converted the rude granite by their deposits into organic matter and new rocks, thus preparing other forms of matter, each one progressing through the heaps of slain. What less than the greed of pay could have kept down the excess of these huge beasts, and what but savage natures have torn and rent and dug and ploughed the world, when man was not to work thus? And so the love of gain and greedy self leads on gold-diggers to sustain a toil which better natures shrink from. Their very evils are the ploughs and harrows by which the gold is won. And then I saw, when monstrous forms were dead, and nature, in organic rocks and soils and vegetation, at last prepared for man, how rude and shapeless was he! So like the gold in mire and quartz embedded, and yet *'twas still the gold.*

"'I saw him when at first the laving river washed off the soil. How the yellow metal, though all unwrought, shone out like rude affection in savages and criminals, and beings who, though unwrought, and bound about with quartz, with hard and rocky sins and stony vices, yet had the gold within! I saw God caring for them, making the proud and wealthy wait upon their labor, send them far and wide, like gold, in ships; and in this very scattering, I saw how order grew out of disorder; how heavy hammers bruised them — the cold world's blows (the prison and the fetter); I saw them show like atoms cut and mashed, borne down by sorrow, beaten, broken-hearted, but yet *the gold was there.* I saw them often, in the dens of vice, lie like the heaps of dust — no use, nor beauty. I saw them in the fire — the fire of struggle, poverty, and hunger. I saw them burn and cool, and burn and cool; and higher yet I traced the various classes; and *all were gold, still gold.* I looked with growing interest upon the noble bars. Ay, these are men, indeed, — these bars of gold,— and yet they are not saints — more fit to strike with man, to toy, or worship — more hammering with trade and commerce. They must be beaten finer with bankruptcy's hard hammer; with sorrow's blows become more soft and fine; the depths within must be ploughed up with grief. Strike hard, O world! the gold is not yet current. The circle of the virtues is not found, until, at last, the keen steel knife of death cuts off the corners of the square world-man, and leaves the circle perfect — a saintly shape, fit for the mint of God! Now stamp it with his image — the regal attribute of love divine, that rules the race; and lo! the God-like man, outwrought from soil and mud and quartz and crime! the golden guinea man! the current coin most valued! the thrice-refined gold spirit! The twilight's gray grows blackness, but through the gloom the page of gold shines out, all love and wisdom. I saw the gold of God within the human soul, in every phase of workmanship. I saw it in the miners, whose very vices were levers to move the whole, and set the work in motion. I saw it in the earth, the quartz, the atoms, dust, and burning fluid, the lump, the bar, — the once, twice, thrice, and hundredth time refined, — still the same gold as in the precious guinea.

"'In tracing up its life, I saw how brains grew big, and minds shone out in efforts to perfect it; how arms grew strong, and muscles hard and mighty, by exercise and labor; the uses of all things — all instruments, all metals, and all woods, machinery, and elemental force — to bring it to perfection. So jails and scaffolds, prison bars and laws, governments and systems, crimes and virtues, sufferings and joys — all, all became machinery, and hammers, fires, crucibles, and axes, knives and descending weights, to coin, at last, the image of a

God, and stamp it on the saintly soul of man. Shall I despise the means, or loathe the gold before it is the guinea? Shall I ask God to create the gold all perfect, stamped, and finished? Ay, that's the word — FINISHED. Were all men guineas born, then life is FINISHED, and that which completes the circle must also end the work. If life is motion, then imperfection is the way, effort the means, suffering the goal, and even vice the motor. Perfection is annihilation, unless it becomes a point where effort ceases only to take breath, and start anew, through higher toils and efforts to attain a higher point, more perfect than the last, but relatively dross, compared with the higher currencies in the ever-growing mints of life eternal. The darkness thickens, but only to display the gorgeous array of silver stars. Night is adversity, on whose black pall the stars of wisdom, patience, kindness, strength, shine out in grandeur, which the day conceals.'

"So spake the guardian spirit, as he closed the page of gold; whilst I, beholding through the darkness how light shone, how value grew from effort, gold from soil, responded meekly, 'Let this fragment tell God's love and justice doeth all things well.'"

Dr. P. B. Randolph's Letter.

High authority on questions of this nature, speaking on the subject now before us says: —

"Unquestionably, all the faculties pertaining to man as we find him on the earth, are the result of his location — here; their function or office is to subserve his own unfolding, and the divine purpose — here; and when by death he is transported elsewhere, other faculties, adapted to his new position, will be duly brought into action. Their germs are in him here; they spring up at death, blossom in the spiritual land, and will bear fruit in that place, and at that period of the eternal year, when God shall see proper to so ordain it. We none of us fairly know what we *are;* and none, not even the highest seraphs, can tell positively what we shall be; yet that man is reserved, and will, through all his trials, be preserved for some great, some undreamed-of destiny or end, there cannot be the shadow of a doubt. I hold that all our knowledge here acquired serves its purpose *here;* the grander, the sweeping, the deathless longings of the soul, are to be gratified somewhere else. What we acquire here is necessarily material, and hence can in nowise affect the nature or volume of the soul itself. Man is really a unitary being, but seemingly is duplex or multiple; but this is seeming only.

"There is but one real sense to man, or in man. That sense is intuition — the human sprout of an infinite and God-like faculty, dormant in most of us, but partially expressed in, or manifested by others, yet incontestibly destined to an immense unfolding in all. Whatever is, is therefore right, so far as the *real* man is concerned; yet I do not think this holds good of his personal *accidents* — using this term in reference to our phenomenal existence here on earth, viewed with man's limited powers of discernment; yet that even these 'accidents,' seen from the standpoint of the Infinite, are absolutely right, it were folly for me to dispute. Reason — the faculty given us here merely as the pilot through life — has fulfilled its office when we step into the grave. When we step out of it, the sense, par excellence, comes into play. This sense is the all-knowing, ever-spreading intuition. This universalizing faculty unquestionably is *not* the product of earthly growth. It is a faculty of prevision and reminiscence. Beyond all doubt the skin of a man is not the man, although whoever sees one, recognizes *something* human. Beneath this skin is the muscular system, with its magnificent network, all in the form, yet by no means the man himself. Beneath this is the osseous system — the skeleton; yet when we see a skeleton, we realize a something pointing toward the human, yet do not for an instant confound the bones with the individual, because we know that *he* is, and to earthly vision ever was and will be, invisible.

"We must look below the skin, muscles, nerves, and skeleton to find the man. Next we find the senses—five, six, or a dozen; yet, although this gets us still nearer the man, we are quite a distance off still. Then come the faculties and tastes;—almost there!—then the lower and higher passions;—not home yet!—then God-like reason and the qualities of virtue, aspiration, and expression; each one step nearer the man! But there is a deep thing just beyond all these, and that thing is intuition—God's omniscience condensed into four square inches of surface. This is the sense, par excellence, of the soul, yet it does not burst into full activity at once, but requires *conditions* for its expansion, just as the faculties require *time* and exercise. My idea is, that the soul is really a divine monad—a particle, if you please, of the eternal brain. It once was *there* as an individual integer; becomes incarnated *here* as an individual, *per se;* and intuition therefore is an *awakening* to a personal consciousness of that which the inmost soul *knew* by reason of its deific genesis The suffering, etc., of man I regard as means adapted to this individualizing; and undoubtedly the faculties and passions are agents to this end also. Evil is the principal agent. We are beset by it on all sides, that we, in shunning it and conserving *self*, may effect the earliest possible completion and rounding out of the inner man.

"Of course, then, I cannot evade the conclusion, looking at the subject as I do from the standpoint of intuition itself, that God knew his business well when he began the world; and therefore, when we take this lofty stand to pass judgment on Dr. Child's philosophy, we cannot help affirming that he is, beyond all cavil, correct when he affirms that 'Whatever Is, is right.'"

The above letter is virtually and really a recognition

of the doctrine of this book; yet my brother Randolph, in his recently published work called "The Unveiling; or what I think of Spiritualism," reasons somewhat with material philosophy, and fires some warlike guns of condemnation at *whatever is, is right.* If he loves to do this, there is a good cause, and it is right that he should. But his beautiful development of intuition sends forth its gleams at times. Then reason and philosophy dwindle to nothingness, and his perception and condemnation of evil fall back and are lost in the light of spiritual truths.

Letter from Mrs. J. S. Adams.

"The philosophy of 'whatever is, is right,' developed, is the only true method of harmonizing the conditional evils of life.

"Spiritual truths are not perceived by the material senses. The mental faculties of mankind, in their present stage of existence, cannot recognize delicately evolved spiritualities; they are too subtile for them to comprehend, and spiritual things are only spiritually discerned.

"This philosophy, therefore, does not admit of argument, it cannot be measured by the formulas of earth, or righteously judged of by the usual method of reasoning; it must come, and can come only intuitively, naturally, to every soul.

"The lives of true men and women are not injuriously affected by its adoption. It does not detract one particle from the strength and growth of a full and vigorous manhood; its aim being to establish harmony in the place of discord.

"A character without what are termed 'faults,' would be most negative and repulsive, and life without evil, so called, would be any thing but desirable—a passive condition wherein virtue would have no reward, truth no merit, and progress no obstacles to aid the spirit's growth.

"Most cordially have I adopted the philosophy of *Right*, and endorsed the spiritual significance of the theory you propose to present to the people in your forthcoming volume.

"I sincerely hope that you may be encouraged and sustained in your noble efforts by the inhabitants of earth, as you have been and now are by the angels of heaven."

The following well-written letter, over the signature of *Lex Naturæ*, is selected from the columns of the *Banner of Light*, and will throw light on the subject of this book:—

"The frequent conflicts of opinion that appear in the *Banner* in relation to the very natural views entertained by Dr. Child, are, no doubt, to him, and perhaps to others who appreciate the full merits of the views expressed by him, a source of amusement, at least in one sense. It is as if some one had propounded an enigma, the solution of which, *when once explained*, is so inevitably apparent, that the wonder is that it required any explanation at all.

"But all men are not endowed with an intuitive appreciation of truth capable of making itself manifest through a thick veil of prejudices, the result of education, or perhaps a 'constitutional predisposition' to error — a sort of hereditary taint. The writer of this article has at various times been 'exercised' mentally on the same points which glitter so clearly in Dr. Child's opinions. I recollect some of the mental phenomena of my childhood, when my intuitions were more clear than they now are, and had not been diverted into unnatural channels; and prominent among the *illustrations* memory affords me of the *key* to some of the *causes* which influence the actions of men, is one of the following character:—

"The subject of predestination had occupied my mind for several days, though I was not old enough to understand the subject by such a name, or any other name. I reasoned with myself, 'Is it possible that every thing which occurs is determined beforehand by the power that created? It is said God knows every thing, made every thing, and governs every thing.'

"And to put my doubts at rest by a test of an experimental character, I set myself to do something I never before thought of doing; and when I had commenced, I stopped suddenly and said to myself, 'I will not do it'—and set myself reasoning again on the matter. And at this point, the first thought that occurred to me was, 'Was it not determined beforehand that I should do as I have, and not do as I have not done?'

"Various exercises, differing in many respects, led me eventually, in very early life, to the conclusion that all phenomena are the result of something going before, of which they were the natural sequence; or, it may be said, all effects are the results of causes, and are inevitable. At a later period, this subject has a more lucid appearance than it had in childhood, for the reason that although my thoughts are less characterized by intuitive phenomena, reason (or the more ordinary methods of thought) is aided by a wider area of facts. And among these facts, the myriad phenomena of Spiritualism are full of evidences; for in all these things may be seen curious evidences of causes which may be clearly inferred in effects of a character full of novelty to the human mind.

"The phenomena of Spiritualism are full of evidence of the *causes* which influence that most perplexing of all subjects of investigation—the human mind. By the aid of our recent acquaintance with Spiritualism, we learn that the human mind is often prompted by unseen agencies in the invisible world, which, because consciousness does not recognize them as such, we too often suppose are merely the workings of our own minds, entirely independent of all control; and because we do not understand these agencies as causes, we deny the legitimate inference which a true knowledge of the facts would elicit; to wit, that all effects are preceded by causes, and are inevitable, or, in other words, predetermined or fore-ordained, etc., etc. This one principle lies at the bottom of Dr. Child's philosophy, *that all causes inevitably produce their legitimate effects;* and could we stand behind the veil that conceals causes from our perceptions and understanding, we could as inevitably predict the results as they would occur.

"There is one principle which many minds that are far advanced in the knowledge of truth, do not recognize; or, if they do recognize it, they do not bring it to their aid in considering the *incidents* which control them in the formation of their opinions, and this principle needs to be frequently set before the vision of the inquirer after truth. It is this: Nature conspires by means to produce results. In other words, nature, by a *general* combination of causes, produces a *general* combination of effects. By strictly excluding particulars and details, *as such*, from consideration, but regarding them in the aggregate, by aggregating causes and by aggregating effects, we see the force of Dr. Child's reasoning.

"But let us isolate examples, and we may not always see the true relation of a single incident to the aggregate, which alone is the true test. To make this more plain, we will bring the matter up in a comprehensive form, so as to admit of demonstration. For example, the meteorologist, in determining the temperature of any particular locality, takes the average of the aggregate of a long series of records of temperature for months and years. Were he, however, to reason as men are apt to, *from a single observation*, or even half a dozen, he would have a hundred chances against arriving at the correct temperature, for one chance for obtaining it. And as it is in this and innumerable other departments of scientific investigation, aggregates and averages are the test of a law of nature; and the same principle exists also as a test of other laws of nature, whether relative to crude rudimental matter, or to matter in its more refined and spiritualized condition associated with the highest function of matter—the development of intelligence."

Charlotte H. Bowen, of Wankegan, Ill., writes to the *Banner of Light* as follows:—

"I have earnestly advocated the principle that 'Whatever *is*, is right,' for many years. I did not learn it from Pope, nor did I understand it when reading him. But when I began to unfold interiorly, this, with many other beautiful ideas, was born within me. Thus I call it an *interior consciousness*—not knowledge of the intellect; for it seems entirely new to me, as though I had never read or heard of it. The influence of these convictions has made me cease condemning any person or action, however vicious. I have been scorned and scoffed at, reviled and persecuted, and called all manner of evil names, for believing as I do; so it need not be wondered at that I rejoice in reading Dr. Child's sentiments. To see one so gifted and capable come out and advocate these beautiful though unpopular truths so fearlessly, melts my heart with emotions of joy and gratitude, not only to him, but to the 'powers that be.'

"There are a 'few wise men,' who have seen the star just risen in the East, and will assemble to worship it, or rather the principle, the 'young Child' over which it stands. So say on, my brother; truth will make you strong, bold, and free. Nothing should make us shrink from the advocacy of truth, when we become fully conscious of its omnipoten(

Lysander Spooner says:—

"Our ideas of good and evil seem to have had their origin in pleasure and pain. Those actions that make us happy we call good, and those that make us unhappy we call evil. We say of things, also, those that give us pleasure are good, those that give us pain are evil. We speak of the weather, and call it good weather or bad weather; of an enterprise, we say it is good or bad, according as its results give us pleasure or pain. From childhood we have learned the causes of pleasure and pain, and have thus distinguished between good and evil. In maturer life we have often found that what produces pain, at first, produces pleasure in the end, and *vice versa.* A virtuous man is one who does not participate in present pleasures when they lead to pain. A vicious man is one who surrenders to temptation for the moment, without regard to the pain that comes in the end.

"Virtue and vice we know only by contrast. Beauty and deformity, light and darkness, heat and cold, we know only by contrast. We know nothing, except by contrast. It is necessary that these contrasts should be perpetually occurring in the natural order of things. It seems to me that it is necessary for us to grow in the knowledge of good and evil.

"As a whole, nothing should be set down as evil, because there is nothing that does not produce greater good than evil, in the end. I think that God caused every thing that we call good and evil.

"As to the effect of this belief on man in his actions, I think it is harmonizing; it takes away blame; it makes all feelings of revenge cease; it makes men see that it is no fault of a wolf that he is a wolf—no virtue of the lamb that he is a lamb."

Miss Fannie M—— writes to the *Banner of Light* as follows:—

"I await with impatient delight your weekly visits, for

you have truly become an indispensable visitor, and I gather much spiritual food from your beautiful truths, among the brightest and most beautiful of which are those contained in the views of Dr. Child. And could they be read with an unprejudiced and liberal mind, I think your readers would perceive in them as much truth and beauty as I do.

"Ask your kind readers to mark his language, his conversation, and see if there be any attempt to assert a belief for others, or even to judge others. No; far from it. I think if people would exercise more magnanimity of soul, more liberality, if they would consider and weigh well his beautiful theory, they would not condemn, but admire its beauty. I admire his liberality, his progressive soul, his divine love for all, and I trust there will be a time when the whole world will look upon humanity with the same loving and progressive spirit."

Miss Lizzie Doten, entranced, says:—

"Evil is evil only by comparison; a lower condition than ours is evil to us, and our condition is evil to a higher condition. It is necessary for the tree that it should begin its growth at the root. The roots grow in the ground in the darkness of the earth; the trunk and branches grow up toward heaven. The roots may be compared to evil, the trunk and top to good; the ramifications of each are similar; both are good, both are necessary. So it is of the soul's growth; every degree is necessary. The nearer we come to God, the purer grows the soul. Why does Dr. Child present such views? It is because the philanthropy of his large heart wants to take all humanity to heaven—the wicked and the suffering, as well as the good and the happy. He would take even the Devil himself to heaven; and it may be that the Devil will have a seat in heaven; that God will say—

"'Take, Lucifer, thy place. This day art thou
Redeemed to archangelic state.'

"The views of Dr. Child are broad and comprehensive; he goes for generals. His views are right; his position is true. In this general view the wisdom of Providence is seen in its perfection; there is no evil, no sin; but when you come to minutiæ, with limited perception, you see evil. God produced every thing good at first, and God has never changed his mind; every thing is good still.

"You are beginning to accept these broader views which are made manifest in the kindness you show to sinners, criminals, and prisoners. This is but the beginning of the good that shall be seen to result from the views this brother advances.

"In machinery there is friction, which makes a loss of power. Evil is the friction of life; it is the conservative power that prevents men from flying off in a tangent to perfection; it is a necessity; it is the regulator of the soul's growth; it times the progress of the soul. The higher the soul rises, the clearer it will see that every condition it has passed has been necessary; and that every condition of life has been good in itself. Generation upon generation shall look back and see that the darkness of the past has been necessary to the condition that produced that darkness."

A correspondent, J. C. W., of the *Herald of Progress*, writes as follows: —

"BROTHER DAVIS: Please be kind enough to give me your impression respecting the views of Dr. A. B. Child on the theory of evil. He declares that every thing is *good*, every thing is *right*, every thing is *beautiful*. Do inform us with your understanding."

A. J. Davis' answer.

"Although Dr. Child is clear in his hopes and thoroughly spiritual in his estimates of existence, yet is he obscure and unsound in that shadowy, metaphysical realm where integral consciousness meets with acquired and sensuous knowledge. And we hold that, in the present sphere of rudimentalism, it is next to impossible to be limpid in all our statements, even when the truth itself ripples through the soul with the transparency of heaven's pure light. Yes, in the highest, widest, truest statement, every thing is *good*, is *right*, is *beautiful*. But this generous statement is for the far-off future, refers to ultimates, anticipates results; and it is not, therefore, practically adapted to the conditions and intermediates of the past or present. Because the finger of wisdom and goodness is visible in every thing, and because there is a world of intelligences environing ours, with which our life and destiny are interlinked and inseparable, it does not follow that every thing is *as* perfect, *as* good, *as* pure, *as* beautiful as it can become, and will be, in the 'far-off future time,' when every germ will have ultimated its properties, and the buds of earth will have bloomed in heaven.

"Progression implies imperfections to be overcome, as action implies rest, day includes night, right covers left, etc.; but universal present perfection annuls the use of any progressive law, and levels all the spirals of *eternal* spheres, which are diversified and constitutionally different, because *unlike* or unequal in their goodness, purity, wisdom, and life. Ultimate truths and final principles, although consoling and exalting to every sentiment of human nature, cannot be *facts* in rudimental life—that is, they cannot embody and describe what is, but only that which is to come.

"In the ultimate statement, then, we harmonize heartily with our brother, but discord comes with the attempt to confound rudimental facts with ultimate principles. This result in logic is easily accomplished; but in fact, in experience, in sensuous knowledge, no such logic is successful. It falls with its own weight or evaporates into air. This life is germinal, and, *as such*, it is 'good, right, beautiful;' but, as compared with a better life, — a state more right and more beautiful, — it falls below those adjectives, and suggests that which is crude, cruel, and evil. Hence our voluntary exertions to make progress toward what is more desirable, or at least, to unfold the present up to the standard of our ideals. Of broadest and ultimate truth the poet hath well said: —

"'Evil is to God what lightning is to light;
Lightning slays *one* thing, light makes *all things* live.
Bear, then, thy necessary ills with grace;
No *positive* estate or principle
Is evil — debtor wholly for its being
And measure to defect — defect to good.
What God directly makes must e'er be good,
And what is good, in whole, or part, he loves,
And must; the others are but off-shoots. *Ill*
Is limited. What pow'r could form a scheme
Of universal evil, or eternal?'"

In answer to the question, "are there no bad spirits?" Mr. A. J. Davis has the following: —

"We do not recognize all spirits, either in this world or the next, as occupying the same relative positions to truth and goodness. Some are ignorant, dark, discordant, and unprogressed; while others are wise, bright, harmonious, and beautiful; but intrinsically (*in the heart and core of life*) we can discover 'no high, no low, no great, no small.' In the *essence* of being all are alike, but the world-wide discrepancies occur in the region of relations; same materials and identical principles, infinitely diversified by difference of combination. We have never taught that all spirits are pure and reliable; but that all are progressing centre-ward."

From the pen of my good brother, A. J. Davis, have flowed a thousand streams of pure inspiration, that have filled my soul, and a million other souls, with ecstacy. If a debt of gratitude I owe on earth, it is for inspired truths given through the organism of Mr. A. J. Davis.

Miss Lita Barney, of Providence, R. I. says: —

"I suppose that Dr. Child will explain in his forthcoming book on good and evil, as the main object, the idea of the use of evil, and how to turn it to our highest good."

I regret that Miss Barney's able pen has not explained this, and that her explanation should not be herein recorded.

I think that what is called evil is a lever in the hands of Infinite Wisdom, to lift the soul from earth to heaven. Conflict and inharmony are warring to destroy earthly love, which love, when conquered, frees the soul from earthly bondage.

Mr. Cushing says: —

"The argument of Dr. Child is logical, and, if true in any part, is true in the whole. He is to Spiritualism what Hume was to the age in which he lived. He is the only consistent reasoner I have heard in the ranks of Spiritualism. But his basis is absolute *fatality*. His position is, that all matter and all worlds are moved by the same Almighty Power; all life, and all the manifestations of life, may be attributed to one great cause. And, consequently, he comes across nothing wrong. From this position, he must conclude that slavery and murder are right, and all crime, and all the curses of the earth; and he has no hand or voice to raise against evil. Ask him what is evil, and he says there is none. Ask him what God is, and he answers, nature. He says cause is nature, and effect is nature; all is right. His position claims that there is no use in trying to correct men, for there is no power to correct wrong; that man is a part of God, and God is infinite. If this position be true, he might as well blot out his manuscripts as to read them; for there is nothing to reason upon. He has made assertions without the least proof to sustain them."

The position that I have taken does not claim that there is no use in trying to correct men; neither does it claim that there is no power to correct what we call wrong. I agree with my brother Cushing, that, so far as concerns the soul, my manuscripts and all other manuscripts may well be blotted out; and further, I agree with my brother, that there will be nothing to reason upon, and no necessity for reason, when intuition is well developed; and further, I agree with my brother, that my assertions find *little* proof in *little* limits.

Mr. Wetherbee says:—

"I am on Dr. Child's side.

"'All nature trembles to the throne of God.'

"'All are but parts of one stupendous whole,
Whose body nature is, and God the soul;
That changed through all, and yet in all the same,
Great in the earth as in the ethereal frame.'

"There are differences in nature; all things are not alike; there is light and darkness, cold and heat, good and evil, as we say. There is a necessity for all these things; the wisdom and power of God in nature produces them. To the vegetable world darkness is just as necessary as light. So to the world of intelligence evil is just as necessary as good; without evil there could be no progress. Evil has given to us a greater part of our intelligence. In a very limited sense, there is evil in the world; but in a broad and comprehensive sense, what is called evil is an absolute good, necessary and essential to human progress. God is perfect. The perception of evil is external and material; and this evil is as transient to the soul as is the use of material things. The material world is a necessity in the early growth of the soul, and so is what we call evil."

Mr. Chaney say:—

"We have been taught that if God were to withdraw his support from us one moment we should fall. If we admit this as a fact, we must admit the truth of Dr. Child's views."

Mr. Chaney also says, in the *Saturday Reporter*, of which paper he is editor:—

"Until recently we have never heard of any person who agreed with Pope in the expression 'Whatever is, is right.' Our attention was first seriously directed to it by A. B. Child, M.D., and, notwithstanding the prejudices of a lifetime, after listening to the Doctor for an hour or two, our reason was convinced, in spite of our prejudice, that those four words embody a mine of truth.

"During the recent convulsion among the churches, brought about by Spiritualism, Dr. Child has been agitating this question, in private conversation, public discussion, and through the columns of the *Banner of Light*. At first his ideas were received with scorn and derision; but, gradually, the prejudice of ages has been yielding, and while many have been hopefully converted to this eternal truth, thousands are on the anxious seat of inquiry."

The following is an extract from a letter published in the *Spiritual Age*, by "M. J. W.":—

"I must confess that I am in love with the broad and comprehensive theory of our good friend, Dr.

Child. A soul that can look out upon the *seeming* discords, irregularities, and sufferings of earth-existence, and see perfect order, harmony, and goodness blending in one grand whole — one who can walk on all calmly, serenely, and securely, amid the *apparent* contradictions and clashings of mind in its various degrees of development — one who can go forth and place the hand of blessing on the head of *every child of humanity* — one who can lift the heart in silent homage to the God that 'worketh in us both to will and to do of his own good pleasure,' while from his own soul streams forth the blessings of Divine love, is already ripe for martyrdom, and the scaffold of public opinion and condemnation *will* be raised high by those who cannot perceive the beautiful truths which lie enfolded in the simple plan of *true progression.* * * * A voice from the deep, deep world of thought within, tells me 'Dr. Child is right.' * * * *

"Dr. Child's theory *is not* and *cannot* be 'a savor of death unto death,' but a comforting faith, building the soul up in its *highest, holiest* hopes—inspiring it with a calm, unshaken trust and confidence in that Father, who is a loving friend *alike to all*, and by divinest means outworks man's highest, noblest destiny."

The following from the pen of L. C. Howe, was published in the *Spiritual Age:* —

"The problem of evil, which of all subjects is most worthy investigation, involves in the mind a mass of principles, that will require ages to elucidate to the comprehension of earth's immortals. Few minds have been found bold and broad enough, to sweep the universe with the clear eye of reason, and proclaim to the world that 'all is good and beautiful.' And though I cannot synonymize the words 'right' and 'wrong' so as to see every thing alike lovely and meritorious, I *do* see *much* beauty where I once saw *none;* and from this I infer that I may yet see goodness where now I see but evil; and who shall say that a large growth may not open to my soul *all* the beauties that dazzle the vision of Dr. Child? Be this as it may, we cannot deny that there is much to learn, ere we can settle this great question, compatible with philosophy, and the moral intuitions of the soul; and hence the able discussions of honest minds which are calling out so many criticisms from various sources, are the very things that we need; and I can but marvel at the manifest disposition of many reformers to stifle free expression with the plea of 'A dangerous doctrine.' This cry has been raised against every new unfoldment from time immemorial. When Jesus first lifted his voice against the murderous dogmas of Moses, and proclaimed mercy and forbearance against revenge and intolerance, saying to the adulteress, 'Neither do I condemn thee,' he was hunted by the church as a 'dangerous' innovator, and, at last, paid the penalty of his beneficence, by an ignominious death.

"When the all-embracing charities of Universalism first sounded the glad tidings of infinite and impartial love to the children of men, the creed-contracted world stood aghast, and trembled in view of this 'pernicious and dangerous doctrine!'

"So, too, when the voice of immortality first broke upon the world in the character of 'spiritual rappings,' and sent the sparkling of free thought flaming through the souls of earth, the slaves of education rallied to the rescue, and attempted to muffle the mouth of heaven, lest her immortal hosts should open a new vein of thought, and lead earth's famishing millions to the feast of freedom and truth! But the time moves on, and no power of earth can stay its progressive march.

"Still that voice is heard, whenever a daring mind utters his boldest and broadest thought; and it may be well that it is so, for it calls out the soul's energies to scan closer, to probe deeper, and prune the subject of all objectionable conditions.

"But let us examine the subject more closely. It is

urged that the doctrine which ignores evil, is doing a ruinous work, plunging many who adopt it into dark and fearful errors! Now, it is very easy to find a subterfuge for selfish and debasing gratifications, when the mind is constantly on the alert for such an excuse; and such minds may attempt a vindication of their course, by involving the noble souls who have opened their liberal ideas to the world with candor and honesty. But where is the philosophy in such self-justification? Are we to surrender our individuality, and attempt to torture our souls into heaven, because a great mind believes that the darkest deeds are fraught with the elements of ultimate felicity? If a man be told that, by plunging into a caldron of boiling oil, he will come out a shining seraph, will he be likely to try the experiment, without first attesting the matter, by his own judgment? If you urge me to drink arsenic, that I may the sooner taste the bliss of Paradise, think you that I should put the cup to my lips? Never! But, if a man *love* vice, nothing short of growth in the moral deportment of his nature can possibly eradicate his proclivity thereto.

"If a man has murder in his heart, is he nearer heaven because he dare not execute it? And, if a man have *not* murder in his heart, can sophistry generate it there? Whoever has not the self-hood to think and to *do* for himself, must *need* bitter experience to develop an individuality. The mind that *does* think and adopt principles for *himself*, will *never* be in danger of the sad disasters complained of. Nature *will be* herself, despite our sophistry; and the only possible way to aid in human development, is to give free scope to the largest and most radical thoughts, and labor to cultivate high and pure feelings in ourselves, that by our daily example and aspiring sympathies, we may carry a perpetual moral tone in our souls, strengthen those who are struggling with organic weakness and trembling in the grasp of alluring vices. Our life consists not so much in what we *do*, as in what we *feel*. It is not the *word* that reaches the soul, but heart-life that is *in* the word. If our inner life be true and pure, we have little to fear from the errors of the head. The soul must first *desire* to do good, and the effort to satiate that desire will be forthcoming.

"Let us labor, then, to stimulate that desire in *ourselves first*, and others will soon catch the flame. The feelings of the heart will soon correct the failings of the head; and, if Dr. Child is theoretically in error, then it behooves us, instead of carping at his 'pernicious influences,' to correct the 'sophistry' by practically demonstrating the difference between right and wrong. To attempt the correction of an error, by proscribing free discussion thereon, is tacitly admitting that that error, with an equal chance, is a match for the truth!"

Letter from Leo Miller.

"Deep down in the core of human life is imbosomed an essence of celestial beauty and perfection — a divinity as *impervious to corruption* as its great Prototype, whose image it is. The voice of this divinity is conscience, which neither wealth, nor fame, nor earthly allurements, can ever bribe to silence; and though its sweet cadence is often lost amid the Babel din of human passion, the soul that inspires it, is what it ever was, and is, and ever will be — a *thought* from the Infinite Spirit!

"That inner life is subject to no moral taint, for it is, verily, 'God manifest in the flesh.'"

Mr. Wilson, says: —

"The views of Dr. Child come nearest to the standard of true Christianity of any I ever heard; they are but a reiteration of the philosophy taught eighteen hundred years ago. The largeness of a heart that can comprehend and utter such views as Dr. Child has advanced, can meet the criminal and say, 'Neither do I condemn thee.' And it can forgive by deeds more than by words. These views, carried out into practical detail, are in harmony with the fundamental teachings of Christ.

"I cannot see the immoral tendency that some believe must flow from such views, but I can clearly see the reverse of this. When they are received, they must give humanity a mastery over immorality; their influence is triumphant over evil; it reaches from hell to heaven. By the possession of these views the soul is armed and charged with a positive power over what is called evil.

"I can only judge of others by myself, and of the influence that these views would have upon others by the influence they have upon me. With these views, I know I cannot intentionally injure another man; and I cannot believe that any person is in a lower hell than I am."

THE VIEWS OF THIS BOOK ARE IN PERFECT HARMONY WITH THE SAYINGS AND PRECEPTS OF CHRIST.

Christ has said, "Blessed are the poor in spirit; blessed are they that mourn; blessed are the meek; blessed are they that do hunger and thirst after righteousness; blessed are the merciful; blessed are the pure in heart; blessed are the peacemakers; blessed are they which are persecuted for righteousness' sake; blessed are ye when men shall revile and persecute you. Rejoice and be exceeding glad for great is your reward in heaven."

There is no condition of human life, then, according to these beautiful words of Christ, that comes not within the circle of the blessed; that has not a great reward in heaven; that is not right.

The poor in spirit are blessed. Who are the poor in spirit? Those who have most deformed, degraded, and feeble development of soul are the poor in spirit. The souls of the self-righteous and the self-excellent, those who think they are more religious and better than others, are small and weak in spirit, are poor in spirit, but have excellent and strong garments of material love which cover and protect their spirits while they are poor and feeble. The poor in spirit are those who have not yet a development of soul large enough to discern the realities of the spiritual world; those who can only see the material world and its philosophies. But the poor in spirit are blessed, says Christ.

Blessed are they that mourn. Who are the mourners? Those who suffer; those who are afflicted; those who have with regret, with sorrow, with tears, lost something that belongs to their earthly existence; those who have committed to the grave the ashes of a dear friend are mourners; those whose homes are wrenched from them by the hand of merciless human law are mourners; those who have lost their earthly riches are mourners; those who have lost a good reputation among men are mourners; those who have lost their freedom are mourners; the convicts and the rebels are mourners; the state prison is filled with mourners for lost repute and lost liberty — and if any house should be dressed all over, inside and out, with black crape, it is the prison-house of mourning prisoners. The courtesan is a mourner; she mourns for her departed virtue, which virtue the sensuous world sets the highest value upon. Regrets, remorse, and agony are frequently the inmates of her mourning soul. She mourns for the loss of that kind recognition, that hearty approval, her mother and her father, her sisters, her brothers, and society once bestowed upon her. The murderer is a mourner. O God, what agony of remorse fills his bosom! How his regrets mourn over the deed that he has done! All "evil" deeds make sufferers, and all sufferers are mourners, and "blessed are they that mourn," says Christ.

Blessed are the meek. Who are the meek? The obedient, the patient, the toiling, the mild, the gentle and the humble. The toiling slave is meek; the faithful laborer is meek; the men and the women that are crushed by material excellence, and made to do the hard work of life, are meek; the humble servants that make our fires, and black our boots, and prepare our food, while we lie at ease, are the meek and the beautiful. Poor men and poor women, who submissively and willingly do all the hard work for the rich men and the rich women, are the lowly, the humble, the obedient; they are the meek and the lovely, whom Christ has said are blessed.

Blessed are they who hunger and thirst after righteousness. Who are these? Every child that lives on earth, with not one single exception. Righteousness is right; righteousness is goodness, the possession of which is happiness. Every soul seeks happiness with a deep and ardent desire. Every step taken by every human soul is a step taken to this end. No one voluntarily walks into pain and suffering; but every one, at all times, in all places, and in all conditions, voluntarily takes a step for happiness. Every soul hungers and thirsts after righteousness, the fruition of which is the desire of all. And "blessed are they that hunger and thrist after righteousness," says Christ.

Blessed are the merciful. Who are the merciful? The compassionate, the forgiving, the sympathizing, the tender, and the kind. The merciful are made so by passing the ordeal of sin, suffering, and affliction. To be merciful always is to see no evil. He who with a sacrifice binds up the wounds of the wounded, and helps to assuage the sufferings of humanity by taking the pain upon himself, is compassionate, is merciful. He who forgives the offences of others, and loves the offender just as well after as before the offence was committed, is merciful. He who sympathizes with the down-trodden, and with the outcast, by practical deeds of goodness, is merciful. The woman who is tender and kind to everybody in every condition of society; who is free from pride, scorn, and condemnation, who, by words and actions in her every-day life, sends forth, in practical deeds, the gushings of a loving, affectionate, and generous heart to all around her, is merciful. It is sin and its consequent suffering that makes us merciful. "Blessed are the merciful," says Christ.

Blessed are the pure in heart. Who are the pure in heart? Those whose love of the earth is broken and fallen off; those whose souls have risen above the shadows of matter into the clear light of spiritual realities; those whose vision by natural development has grown to see the hand of God distinct in all things; those who can see God and see no evil. What makes us pure in heart? Travelling through the progressive journey of our earthly life; passing through the fires of affliction; involuntarily drinking the cup of bitterness which wisdom holds to our lips, and which cup is made of sin. The pure in heart are those whose love of earthly things, by affliction and suffering, is torn and stripped off from the soul. The pure in heart are those whose vision sees all things pure, sees all things good, sees that whatever is, is right. "Blessed are the pure in heart," says Christ.

Blessed are the peacemakers. Who are the peacemakers? Those who have done making war; those whose deeds now make peace; those who oppose nothing; no belief, no doctrine, no creed, no pursuit or effort of others; those who fight not any thing or anybody, but those whose souls are in harmony with all life; those whose souls have gained a triumph over the conflicts of the material world by passing through its afflictions, its sin, and its suffering. It is those who can understand the harmony of discord, and see that whatever is, is right. "Blessed are the peacemakers," says Christ.

Blessed are they which are persecuted for righteousness' sake. Who are persecuted for righteousness' sake? All that have suffering on earth. All suffering is a persecution for the sake of happiness; all pain and all affliction is a means in the ordering of nature to bring happiness to the soul. All the afflictions of life are the persecutions of nature, which humanity cannot avoid. But blessed are all they that suffer persecution for the sake of the righteousness, the goodness, and the happiness that shall be theirs in consequence.

Blessed are ye when men shall revile you and persecute you. Who are reviled and persecuted by men? All, to whom the finger of scorn, ignominy, and condemnation is pointed. The man on the gallows; the man in handcuffs and in iron chains; the man in the prison-house; the courtesan; the inhabitants of North Street, the Five Points, and Billingsgate; the man or the woman who steps into a ditch of immorality; the drunken man in the gutter; the man whom *men* "turn out of the church of Christ;" the reformer; the man who presents a new thought to humanity; the man who treads on untrodden ground, who dares to take one step outside the well-beaten path where millions have trod before him. Our beautiful Christ was nailed to the cross for this; was on that cross reviled and persecuted by men. And he has said, "Blessed are ye when men shall revile you and persecute you. Rejoice and be exceeding glad, for great is your reward in heaven."

The basis of these teachings of Christ is a palpable recognition of the transcendent reality of the soul which grows up through all the conditions of life, and in *every* condition, without *one single* exception, IS BLESSED. Every condition of life is a pathway peculiar to itself, in which every traveller is ever moving on to one great, grand ultimate — the goal called heaven; to the home of the blessed; to the places prepared for them in our Father's house of many mansions.

Christ has said, Resist not evil. While the soul is conscious of the existence of evil, it is inevitable not to resist it. There is a condition of spiritual development, in which there are no shadows of earth to obstruct the vision of the soul, where no evil is seen; then the soul can obey Christ, resist not evil. No one can obey this command of Christ without acceptance of the beautiful truth, all is right.

Christ says, "Love your enemies, bless them that curse you." How can we love our enemies while we esteem them wrong and evil? We cannot love what we esteem evil. We can only love them by esteeming every manifestation of their hatred and cursing as being a necessary result of a lawful condition; as being a manifestation of goodness in the ordering of Divine Wisdom. In this view we can love them, and bless them. Christ says, "Take no thought for your life, what ye shall eat, or what ye shall drink; nor yet for your body, what ye shall put on. Is not the life more than meat, and the body than raiment?" God feeds the fowls of the air, and clothes the grass of the fields, and shall he not much more clothe you? "Seek ye first the kingdom of God and his righteousness, and all these things shall be added unto you."

In these words of Christ is a foreshadowing of a perfect faith in God; a perfect confidence in the working of all the laws of nature, human action and human effort being a law of God and an operation in nature. These words of Christ recognize the fact of human destiny, absolute fatalism, which is nothing short of perfect trust in God.

In the precepts of Christ is embodied universal blessedness, and the doctrine of unmeasured beauty — Whatever is, is right.

Christ was a friend of the whole human family — of harlots, courtesans, publicans, and sinners, and all the company of hell, for he said — "Come unto me all ye that labor and are heavy laden, and I will give you rest." The spirit of undying love glowed in his breast for all who needed compassion, and more for all those who suffered most. We think that devils suffer more than angels; and for devils Christ's love was deepest and brightest, because such most needed his love.

The inevitable effect of the acceptance of the "all-right" doctrine, is to follow Christ's example in the exercise of compassion, sympathy, and kindness for the suffering, the miserable, and the down-trodden of the earth.

The precepts of Christ, and his manifestation of life, stand out, to my preception, more palpably *spiritual*, than the precepts and manifestations of any man I know on the pages of profane or sacred history.

The power of love was so great in Christ, that it has moved the hearts of men for two thousand years as no power has ever done.

WHAT EFFECT DOES THE DOCTRINE, "WHATEVER IS, IS RIGHT," HAVE UPON MEN AND SOCIETY?

What effect does the soul have upon men and society that has a condition developed which can see the hand of God in every thing; that can see beauty in all life; that can, from its deepest convictions, unreservedly declare that whatever is, is right; that evil is good; that both evil and good are God made manifest? The effect of such a soul, in a material sense, upon everybody and every thing that comes within the sphere of its influence, and feels its influence, is to produce heaven. Such a soul has light in which it can see the machination of natural darkness; it can discern the hidden springs of physical laws; it can read the human heart, its intents, designs, and purposes; it can see the God-power beneath, that produces *all* the manifestations of human life. It has grasped what sages and philosophers, poets and divines, have reached for with life struggles, and have longed to grasp; it has found the key to the mysteries of physical life; it sees God in every thing. Such a soul, too, has a power that transcends all the powers of matter combined. It is conscious of a power that matter cannot influence, oppose, injure, break, or destroy. It realizes a power of its own, that rises triumphant above all the antagonisms of earth and the philosophies that belong to it. It is as free as the air of heaven. It is as peaceful as an infant child. Combat such a soul with the war of unkind words, and they have no more effect than the firing of cannon balls would have, made of soap bubbles; such a soul is not hit or hurt by the *religious warriors* of time. Prison bondage has no effect upon such a soul, for the soul cannot be confined. Disease has no effect; every pang is but hastening the object of its longings. To such a soul death is a trivial affair; death is but an incident that comes between the pulsations of the progress of the human soul; a quicker breath, a little damp upon the brow, and the garments of the first minute of life (viz., time) are dropped, are changed for those of the next minute, which time we have supposed was the beginning of our spiritual existence. Such a soul has learnt that the material body was only a garment of spiritual childhood, and that the thorns of life, as we journey on, were made to scratch it off, and give place to new garments adapted to its advanced condition. The thorns and the thistles of life we thought were evil, while in the light of truth we see that they are useful instruments — shears, scissors, and ripping knives, that cut our earthly garments away; the lesser affections of the soul that bind it to matter and make it sooner free; and the deeper and stronger affections of the soul for things above are sooner developed; which affections make the new garments of spiritual existence far more lovely, far more beautiful than the garments of the earth, the physical body.

The whole idea, that the world is all wrong, that all things are wrong, that men are what they ought not to be, and things are not what they should be, fades out of the soul's consciousness, and, like the illusion of phantoms, is gone, leaving no real traces of the existence of evil behind. And all life comes up clothed in new beauty; for the soul has broader conceptions; worlds of new truths open to its deeper perceptions; stars shine with a new lustre; planets revolve in the order of a new creation, and new perceptions of the eternal God go out in the light of undimmed reality. The horizon of human love grows as broad as the conceptions of the soul; and beauty is seen emanating from the heart of life through every thing that has existence — through deformity no less than through symmetry — through evil no less than through good — and the soul has come to see God by its natural growth, through the avenues of the love of Christ, the Jesus of Nazareth.

In the light in which no evil is seen, every human soul appears immortal; and the real recognition of the property of immortality in a human soul is enough; the beauty is too great; it staggers our feeble powers of endurance to behold it; it stifles our utterance, if we attempt to describe it; it is too mighty for our consciousness to weigh. And it is here we cease to weigh the merits and the demerits of another soul; here we cease to judge. The possession of the properties of eternal life and eternal progress belongs to every soul, with no exceptions, if it belongs to one. This simple truth, when realized, is brighter than the material sun that shines upon us at noon-day, in the light of which no shadows of the night of evil can be seen. In the light of these truths, the soul sees and values the real thing — not the effect, which is but darkness, and passeth away — or the soul comes up through it.

In every-day practical life, these views, if reached fully, annihilate hell and open heaven. The enmity of the soul ceases; bitter feelings cease; seeming faults in others disappear; slander and calumny are no more; a war of words is ended; getting mad, and being contentious is done with; war is ended, murder is ended, both legal and illegal; robbery, both legal and illegal, is ended; the curses of prostitution, both legal and illegal, are ended; bondage is ended, and freedom has commenced. Human souls fall into the arms of spontaneous love, that comes of natural growth. This development will make men always kind and friendly to one another; it will make men religious, by being spontaneous and natural in all their actions, true to the dictates of reason and common sense; it opens the book of nature for our Bible, and we read with understanding, and learn by natural development.

A soul that can see no evil, no wrong, sees some good and admirable qualities in every one, even in the most repulsive; and these apparently small, dim developments of goodness, when gazed at intently, become so luminous as to make the darkest soul look bright and beautiful; and it is this light of goodness that we may, in every one, always see, when we have the capacity to do so, that destroys repulsion, and burns away all the shadows and darkness of what might otherwise be counted sin or evil.

A soul that sees no evil, sees goodness and beauty everywhere, in every thing. It has no fault to find, no opposition to make, no war to sustain, no hell to combat — all is peace, all is charity, all is love. You ask what influence a man has upon society, whose soul is developed so as to see that all God's works are right? Why, I cannot but repeat, that heaven is wherever he goes. His faith in God is without limits; his charity for others is as broad as the household of humanity, and the kingdom of heaven is within his bosom.

Is such a man as this a bad man in society? Are we afraid of such a man as this? Henry Ward Beecher says that he is afraid of such a man as this, or of a man that says that it is not wrong to steal. And many others are afraid, when they hear the truth declared in unqualified words — "*There is no evil.*" The fear of the Lord is the beginning of wisdom; this fear is right and in its right place. But we shall all sometime see, as we grow in spirit and in truth, that *there is no evil* — then there will be no fear. Perfect love casteth out all fear; a growth of soul that is capable of seeing God's hand in sin, does not, cannot fear it.

A man who sees no evil is a guardian angel to human suffering; he walks with the lowly and talks with them; he is *en rapport* with the most degraded souls, so called — souls most infantile in spiritual growth. Infant children have the guardian care of angels and seraphs. And so it is with the souls of men — infants in spirit — buried deepest in the darkness of the material world; they have the love of God, through his angels and seraphs, to hold, nurse, protect, guide, and direct them, unseen, in darkness, through all the childish, or as we do say, evil, manifestations of early existence.

A man who sees no evil, does not, cannot wrong another; he is faithful and honest in all the duties of life. He needs no government of human law to make him do to others as he would that others should do to him; he never uses human law to protect self-possessions. He needs no locks, no guns, no prison walls; no human legislation, no executive, no human tribunals, no courts of justice, no human judges. He earns his bread by the sweat of his brow. He does the work of life peacefully, honestly, truly, humbly. All hail that day! when humanity shall see in soul, that all that is, is right, for then peace shall reign over the whole earth.

THE LILY WREATH

OF SPIRITUAL COMMUNICATIONS;

Received chiefly through the Mediumship of Mrs. J. S. Adams, by A. B. Child, M.D.

Those who have read this work pronounce it unsurpassed in purity and elegance of diction, in beauty and simplicity of style, and in its correct and attractive presentation of truth. It is printed in a superior manner, equal to that of the finest annuals, bound in rich and durable binding, and in every way made, in typographical and mechanical appearance, in keeping with the intrinsic value of its contents. From numerous notices of the work, the following are selected as expressive of the general opinion respecting it: —

These heavenly colloquies impart truer joys, deeper convictions, and holier aspirations to the heart, than all the dry abstractions and subtle formulas of metaphysical ratiocination that have eclipsed the world. They send out nectar-draughts to the thirsty soul. The young, the aged, will drink and be inspired; and every supply will quicken and beautify the plants of truth, love, and goodness, that vegetate in the garden of the heart. These pages will speak words of progressive cheer to every saddened and earthward mind; utter great truths, with persuasive power, to myriads in error and doubt; breathe soft music over the distressed and harrassed soul; open the portals of immortality to the scorner and sceptic; impart comfort and consolation to the grieved and afflicted, and bring the evidences of angelic presence home to the credulity of our age.

The entire volume breathes the spirit of devotion to a higher life than is known to mortals, while affection and sympathy are ever knocking at the door of our better nature for fellowship and acceptance. We would say to our friends who wish to bestow a beautiful, and at the same time a *pure* present, let the "Lily Wreath" be your selection.

No one can have any just idea of the contents of this volume until they have perused it. The revelations consist in advice, encouragement, and admonitions, couched in language the most chaste and original. The whole book seems to be written in an earnest and truthful manner, and inculcates the purest and most exalted piety.

A correspondent of a Boston paper writes as follows: For every person it possesses a value above the ordinary publications of our time. To the mourner it imparts consolation; the weary it inspires with hope; to the troubled soul it whispers peace; to the sinful soul it speaks in tones of loving, tender earnestness, and to the religious of all classes it offers pure, unsullied Christianity. We would say to all, if you wish to be holier, happier, and nobler, by all means read and ponder the beautiful teachings of this book.

A lofty and ethereal strain of sentiment—a vein of deep, spiritual feeling—pervades the book. The style is quiet, easy, and full of pensive beauty, "winding like a river at its own sweet will;" and the contrast it presents to the hurry and vehemence visible in many publications of the day is like that which one experiences on leaving the hubbub and heat of the city in August, for the delicious quiet and coolness of a grotto.

The evidence of its spiritual origin is furnished by the angelic purity which beams forth from its pages. It will furnish the reader with many interesting and beautiful conceptions of the spirit-life, and of the office and influence of guardian spirits over mortals.

It is a remarkable production; and, as a readable, religiously inclined production, has no equal.

It contains a philosophy whose purity, rationality, and elevated, spiritual tone, cannot but commend itself to every ingenuous mind.

It is pure inspiration; a stream of beauty.

A religious gift-book of superior merit.

PRICE, - - - - - - - - - - - - - - $0.75.

BERRY, COLBY, & CO., 3 1-2 Brattle Street, Boston.

THE BOUQUET

OF SPIRITUAL FLOWERS:

Received chiefly through the Mediumship of Mrs. J. S. Adams, by A. B. Child, M.D.

The "Lily Wreath" was received with so much favor by the lovers of spiritual truth, that in compliance with the wishes of many individuals, a continuation is issued under the name of "The Bouquet."

The flowers that form this Bouquet have been gathered in celestial gardens. They are fragrant with angel love, and arranged in the glowing tints of angel pencillings. Delicately must we touch them, and susceptible to the purest spirituality must they be who would fully enjoy and justly appreciate their many beauties.

In each message, let each one consider himself as personally addressed, for to all those who while on earth would catch the tones of angel voices, and the soft notes of golden harps moved to melody by angel hands, this Bouquet is presented as a token of that love which is drawing us *all* home to peace and joys eternal.

Price of each volume, in cloth, bevelled edge, emblematically embossed, - - $0.75.
" " " " " " " " half gilt 1.00.

BELA MARSH, Publisher, 14 Bromfield Street, Boston.

ARCANA OF NATURE;

OR,

THE HISTORY AND LAWS OF CREATION.

Our bark is Reason; Nature is our guide.

By HUDSON TUTTLE.

PRICE, - - - - - - - $1.00.

BOSTON:
BERRY, COLBY, & COMPANY.
Banner of Light Office
1860.

www.ingramcontent.com/pod-product-compliance
Lightning Source LLC
LaVergne TN
LVHW050525100826
845148LV00002B/437

* 9 7 8 1 4 2 5 5 2 0 9 5 3 *